LIFE WITH GOD

by
Herman C. Theiss
A Manual for the Christian Instruction of Adults

Seven Hills Publishers
Seattle, Washington

Cover: Ken Casey
Bible Quotations used by permission from The Revised Standard Version of the Bible, copyrighted 1946, 1952
© 1971, 1973

The Small Catechism by Martin Luther in Contemporary English is copyright © 1960 by Augsburg Publishing House, Board of Publication of the Lutheran Church in America, and Concordia Publishing House, and is used by permission.

Published by Seven Hills Publishers
P.O. Box 99313
Seattle, Washington 98199

Manufactured in the United States of America

Copyright © 1988
by
Herman C. Theiss

10 9 8 7 6 5 4 3 2 1

Life with God

To My Life's Companion

CONTENTS

PREFACE

Life with God was written for the instruction of adults who are interested in becoming members of the church, specifically the Lutheran church. Its aim is to acquaint newcomers with the Lutheran understanding of the biblical message, with Lutheran church practices and, beyond this, to promote the Christian life. It is also widely used as a textbook for individuals and groups, such as Bible classes, Sunday School teachers, church leaders and members concerned about a fresh restudy of Christian fundamentals, a deeper commitment to their Lord, and being equipped to share their Christian faith with others.

The title *Life with God* alerts us to the truth that Christian instruction relates not only to a way of thinking but also to a way of living. It has horizontal as well as vertical dimensions. It describes a right relationship with God which results in right relationships with people, with the church and with the physical universe. The person who lives through faith in Christ is a complete child of God, equipped for every good work.

Life is the word that Christ himself most frequently used to describe his mission. It occurs some thirty times in the sayings of Jesus in the Gospel of St. John. He sums up his message in the words, "These things are written that you may believe that Jesus is the Christ, the Son of God, and that believing you may have life in his name." Yet it is not just Johannine theology. The life motif runs through the whole Bible, from the creator of life in Genesis to the tree of life in Revelation. The dimensions of life in the biblical sense will be explored in the lessons of this book, as a glance at the chapter headings will reveal.

Believing that it is the business of Christian prophets, or teachers, to point out the imps that bedevil the church in their day, excursions are made in *Life with God* to deal with unbiblical ideas and behavior that are widespread both within and outside the church. While pointing to Christ, "the way, and the truth, and the life," we must take the precaution of posting signs against "the way that seems right to a person, but its end is the way of death." These things are written, too, so that, in the words and by the power of our Lord Jesus Christ, you may have life and have it abundantly.

Two lessons have been added in this fourth revision without, however, adding substantially to the length of the book. Lessons one and four in previous editions, which contained more material than could be handled in single lessons, were divided to make all lessons of relatively equal length. The printing out of many relevant Bible passages which were formerly referred to by chapter and verse did add to the length of the book but will be timesaving for its readers.

Acknowledgments

The author is indebted to many fellow-pastors for the contents of this book. He is particularly grateful to Dr. Richard Caemmerer, his former classmate, for his encouragement, support and helpful suggestions. Dr. Walter Rubke offered much needed help in the area of pedagogy. Many of the constructive criticisms of Pastors Edwin Sohn and Paul Theiss have been incorporated into the text of this fourth edition.

Improvement in the format and, occasionally, the text should be credited to the competent and painstaking work of my editor, Ronn Talbot Pelley.

The author is also grateful to those who offered criticisms which he pondered but did not heed. One such criticism of *Life with God* is that the author sometimes loses sight of his theme. He acknowledges the digressions but does so without any great sense of guilt. There are "things given," such as the Christian creeds, The Small Catechism, the liturgy, that cannot be ignored in a book such as this nor be rewritten to conform to a theme. Generally, the digressions are a tribute to the truth that no single theme can embrace the total Christian message. The motif is not a tyrant. It is a servant that packs the bag for the journey and puts into it whatever fits. Separate bundles must be made for whatever else must go along.

INTRODUCTION

Folks, I would like to introduce you to the church.

Some of you may smile and say, "We are old friends." Others may say a little sadly, "We met before, some time ago. I don't suppose that you remember me." Still others may say, "I am pleased to make your acquaintance," but with the reserve of a person on a first date who has some hesitancy about becoming deeply involved.

YOUR QUESTIONS ABOUT THE CHURCH

Now that we are on speaking terms, what shall we talk about? Whether you are an old friend of the church, a former friend or a stranger, you undoubtedly regard yourself as an inquirer. You have questions to address to the church about its teachings and practices. Many of them, we hope, will be answered in the course of our discussions. It will rest with you to bring up for discussion the unanswered questions which may trouble you. We hope you will do so.

Much more, however, is involved in this conversation than your asking questions and the church trying to answer them. The church is never satisfied simply to answer a person's questions. It also has questions to put to you.

THE CHURCH'S QUESTIONS ABOUT YOU

Your question may be, "Who are these Lutherans?" The question the church proposes is, "Who and what are you in the eyes of God?" Your questions may relate to affiliation with a church organization. "Shall I join? What will be required of me? What do I stand to gain by it?" The church is concerned about your relationship to God upon which all other relationships depend.

Many regard the church as being like a supermarket, of which there may be many in the vicinity. Before people set out to shop they make up a list of the things they want to buy. People also come to the church with a shopping list. They have definite ideas about what they want to get out of joining the church. They may seek affiliation for business reasons, for sociability, for mental or physical health, to please a spouse or relative, to gain the feeling of importance and security that results from belonging to a respectable group, or to resolve a temporary crisis. The concern of the church is the problem of sinful people coming into a right relationship with God, the owner of the supermarket, the dispenser of "every good endowment and every perfect gift." The supreme gift of God, without which not even heaven would be desirable, is God himself: his fatherhood, his lordship over our lives, his fellowship. Before we can expect favors from God we must find favor with God.

This both justifies and explains our topic, *Life with God*, which implies the enjoyment of God's favor. This is the topic given to the church by its Lord. It has no choice in the matter. It must bring to people the message of him who says, "This is eternal life, that they know thee and the only true God, and Jesus Christ whom thou hast sent." (John 17:3)

A MATTER OF LIFE AND DEATH

Life is the word which Jesus most frequently used to describe his mission and work. "I came that they may have life, and have it abundantly." (John 10:10) "Whoever lives and believes in me shall never die." (John 11:26)

By the very choice of the word *life* our Lord alerts us to the grave importance of what he has to say to us. *Life* is the most important word in our vocabulary. Everything we do is directly or indirectly related to warding off death and enjoying life. Our Lord's conversation with us is a matter of life and death.

WHAT BEING ALIVE MEANS

We are bound to ask what our Lord means by the words *life* and *death*. How can he say to people who are alive, "I come to bring you life"? What is the meaning of his promies, "If you live and believe in me you shall never die"? Obviously, what he means by life and death must be something very different from what we commonly understand by these words. What new meaning, or what old meaning that we have lost, does Jesus give to the words *life* and *death*?

Life to him is not mere existence, a pulse, blood coursing through the veins, color in the cheek. To him life never means less than a right relationship with God, living under, with and for God, the enjoyment and practice of his fatherly forgiveness and love.

WHAT BEING DEAD MEANS

Death, in the language of our Lord, is something far more dreadful than the lack of a heartbeat. It is having no heart for God, shutting him out of one's life. It is saying in countless ways, "I want to be independent of God and live my own life." The Bible calls this behavior sin. "The wages of sin is death." (Romans 6:23) The payment for not wanting God (sin) is not having God (death).

The need for God, of which people may not be aware, is the emptiness which accounts for many of their anxieties. Feelings of loneliness, inadequacy, futility, guilt, fear and shame are related to godlessness. Not casting their cares on God they are crushed beneath their weight. Apart from God, from whom, through whom and to whom are all things (Romans 11:36), life has no meaning or purpose. Having no share in God's work, what they do is unimportant. Not knowing God's love and forgiveness, they are victims of guilt and shame. With no God to trust, they are afraid. Death in the biblical sense is a state of inner conflicts, nagging guilt and haunting fears.

St. Augustine summed it up in the words: "The soul was made by God and never finds rest until it rests in God." Of course, no one is wholly free from anxiety because no one wholly trusts in God.

One should not expect people to make this diagnosis of their problems. Our concern is the judgment of God with whom we need to be on right terms. He decreed that "the soul that sins shall die." (Ezekiel 18:20) This judgment makes sense to us only when we know that God is our true Father. We readily understand the father who says of his wayward son who has left home and shut his father out of his life, "My son is dead." Our heavenly Father says of people who have shut him out of their lives, "These my children are dead." "This my son is dead" is precisely what the father said of the prodigal son who chose to leave home and live as he pleased. (Luke 15:11-24)

JESUS WAS TRULY ALIVE AND SHARES HIS LIFE WITH US

Only one person ever truly lived—with and under God, in perfect fellowship and harmony with him. That was Jesus, the true Son of God. Only he could say, "I and the Father are one." (John 10:30)

Jesus offers to share with us the life that was and is in him. It is an offer of God's forgiveness and fatherly love. It is the promise of a meaningful, purposeful life. It is power to love and serve God and people as he loves and serves us. It is the beginning of eternal life which physical death will not terminate. "Neither death nor life...will be able to separate us from the love of God in Christ Jesus our Lord." (Romans 8:38-39)

All our discussions will be related to this subject of life with God through Christ, as the chapter headings in this book indicate. As we proceed we shall see many far-reaching implications of this biblical life-death concept. For the present we shall point out just one.

PEOPLE HIDE—GOD SEEKS

Religion is commonly regarded as an activity that begins with people. It is often defined as a person's search for God. The Bible rules out any such activity on the part of people by saying that they are "dead through sin." It tells the story of God's search for people. The God of sacred scriptures is the giver of life. He is the converter who turns people about, the regenerator who performs the miracle of a new birth by which a person enters the kingdom of God. (John 3:3-6) If a person's religious problem may be compared to the children's game of hide-and-seek, then God is "it."

May he win the game with us by finding us and showing himself to us as our loving Father who has a wonderful life to share with us.

LIFE IS KNOWING GOD
AND JESUS CHRIST

PREVIEW

Life with God requires having a knowledge of God. What, according to the Bible, does it mean to know God? How does a person acquire the knowledge of God? Why must our knowledge of God depend on his self-revelation and not on our religious opinions? What is God's word in its primary sense? Why is Christ called the Word? These are the questions we shall discuss in this lesson.

Knowledge of God Is Life

To enjoy life with God we must know not only that there is a God but also who God is, what he is like and what he did and still does for us as our Creator and Life-giver. Christ said, "This is eternal life, that they know thee the only true God, and Jesus Christ whom thou hast sent." (John 17:3) Not knowing God is death.

The knowledge of God which spells life is not only a matter of the intellect but also of the heart. It describes a right relationship with God. It is knowing God the way loving children know their loving father. It does not exclude knowing important things about their father. But it is much more than this. Rebellious children may know many things about their father, but their factual knowledge serves no good purpose. It is useless, dead knowledge. The concern of the Bible is about an intimate, practiced knowledge of God which never means less than living harmoniously with and under God, trusting him and willingly keeping his commandments. "By this we may be sure that we know him, if we keep his commandments." (1 John 2:3) "He who does not love does not know God; for God is love." (1 John 4:8)

Here again, as with the words *life* and *death*, the Bible writes its own definition. In our language, knowledge relates almost exclusively to facts known about someone or something. When we say, "I know Mr. Smith," we may mean no more than that at some time in the past there was a crossing of paths or that we can recall having heard a few things about him. In the Bible, knowing God is a matter of the heart as well as of the mind, of love and trust and not merely intelligence, of experience and companionship and not hearsay.

How Can God Be Known?

How can we attain the knowledge of God that spells life? There are only two possibilities: either God has made himself known to us and we trust his word or we must depend on our reason and imagination to discover the truths about God.

REASON, A POOR GUIDE

If the latter is true, we are in a bad way. Reason is a precious gift to be used and treasured, but it is wholly inadequate for a right knowledge of God. This is so for two reasons.

First, because of the greatness of God and the limited powers of our reason. After thousands of years humankind is just beginning to comprehend something of the immense but finite universe. What is the hope of science or philosophy discovering the truth about its infinite creator? It really is most reasonable to conclude that the creator of our reason cannot be the product of our reason. If we worship a god our mind has pieced together we are only worshiping ourselves. There must be a better way of formulating a religious creed than by beginning with the familiar words, "I think."

Second, human reason has been corrupted by sin. Pride and guilt distort people's ideas of God. The product of a corrupt mind will be a corrupt god. The god people create is often scarcely more than an enlarged image of themselves, possessing the virtues they admire and the faults they condone. God says, "You thought that I was one like yourself." (Psalm 50:21) That implies, "How wrong you were!" The God of the Bible is the wholly other.

GOD'S SELF-REVELATION

Fortunately, people need not draw their own picture of God. He has made himself known to them through his word. As people communicate with one another by means of words, so God is said to communicate with people through his word. The expression, "The word of the Lord," occurs over 400 times in the Bible.

What is meant by the word of God? Common understanding must regard God and word as incompatible concepts. "God is spirit," as Jesus said. (John 4:24) Words have physical qualities. We cannot expect to hear God's voice or see his handwriting. God's word, therefore, is bound to be something very different from human words. Human words are symbols. God's word is more than a symbol, or sound, or a combination of letters of the alphabet. In its primary sense God's word means an act of God or an event caused by God. As Luther said, "God speaks things not words."

THE WORD OF GOD—A POWER

The power of words depends in a large measure on the person who is speaking. When a military officer says "Come!" and "Go!" the people under him, as Jesus said, come and go. (Matthew 8:5-9) A private could bark out the same commands and nothing would happen. When God speaks, things happen. "The world was created by the word of God." (Hebrews 11:3) "God said 'Let there be light'; and there was light." (Genesis 1:3) The word of God upholds the universe. (Hebrews 1:3) The word of God accomplishes that which he pleases. (Isaiah 55:11)

Because God speaks things it is not possible to separate God's words from his works. Nature, which is God's creation, is a word of God which reveals something about him. "The heavens are telling the glory of God; and the firmament proclaims his handiwork. Day to day pours forth speech, and night to night declares knowledge. There is no speech, nor are there words; their voice is not heard; yet their voice goes out through all the earth, and their words to the end of the world." (Psalm 19:1-4)

God's acts of judgment against the sins of people are his words. "The nations rage, the kingdoms totter; he utters his voice, the earth melts." (Psalm 46:6) Children of God speak of events and experiences as God's word. Their common response to happenings is, "God has spoken."

CHRIST, THE WORD

The Bible calls Christ the Word. (John 1:1-14) This name is most appropriate for him. Words are means of communication. By words we reveal to others what is hidden in us. The true nature of God, especially his amazing love for the sinful human race, is most clearly brought to light in the person and work of Christ, his Son. By his life on earth, which people could see, Christ made the unseen God known to them. "No one has ever seen God; the only Son, who is in the bosom of the Father, he has made him known." (John 1:18) The author of Hebrews says, "In many and various ways God spoke of old to our fathers by the prophets; but in these last days he has spoken to us by a Son.... He reflects the glory of God and bears the very stamp of his nature." (Hebrews 1:1-3) It was not only by his teachings that he made God known but also, and even primarily, by what he was and did and suffered.

Christ also fits the description of the word of God as a creative, life-giving power. By his word he healed the sick and raised the dead. In his pre-human existence he participated in God's work of creation. "He was in the beginning with God; all things were made through him, and without him was not anything made that was made." (John 1:2-3) He upholds the universe by his word of power. (Hebrews 1:3) Through him God creates (brings into existence) his people. "To all who received him, who believed in his name, he gave power to become children of God." (John 1:12) He has power to raise people from the death of sin to life with God. He said, "I am the resurrection and the life; he who believes in me, though he die, yet shall he live, and whoever lives and believes in me shall never die." (John 11:25-26) The knowledge of God which spells life depends on knowing Jesus Christ.

The word of God which is God's activity in creating and sustaining the universe answers questions about the existence and power of God. "Ever since the creation of the world his invisible nature, namely, his eternal power and deity, has been clearly perceived in the things that have been made." (Romans 1:20) His acts of judgment which inflict punishment on people reveal his justice and displeasure with sin. "Is not my world like fire, says the Lord, and like a hammer which breaks the rock in pieces?" (Jeremiah 23:29) Christ, the word made flesh, is God's answer to the all-important question: "How can we sinful creatures know a gracious and forgiving God with and under whom we can live as true children?" "Grace and truth came through Jesus Christ." (John 1:17) Grace means God's surprising, forgiving and undeserving love for people. Truth, related to grace, means there can be no doubt about the trustworthiness of God's love revealed in Christ.

To the list of words and terms which have a largely unfamiliar meaning in the Bible must be added *"word of God."* It means much more than the printed words of the Bible, which is best described as words about the word of God. The word of God is primarily God's creative power that brings life out of nothing or out of death, makes his people those who were not his people, as he did with the children of Israel in Old Testament times, and as he still does for believers in his Son, Jesus Christ.

How can God be known? Through his word. What, in its primary sense, is the word of God? It is God's life-giving power, exercised and seen most clearly in Christ, his Son. He is the word we must know, and come into a trusting relationship with, to enjoy life with God.

Talking It Over

Use each of the following statements and questions as a basis for discussion.

1. What is the church's concern about people? How does it relate to the concern of people seeking affiliation with the church?

2. —the biblical meaning of life and death

3. —why true religion cannot be defined as people searching for God

4. Compare the biblical concept of the knowledge of God with what we mean when we say, "I know Mr. Smith."

5. —the necessity of a religion of revelation (God making himself known)

6. God communicates with people through his word. What is the word of God in its primary sense? Why and how must it be distinguished from human words?

7. What is meant by saying that God speaks things not words?

8. Why is Christ the ultimate word of God?

9. —the all-important question for which Christ is the answer

True and False Statements

Circle the letter **T** for true statements and the letter **F** for false statements.

The purpose of these statements is to provoke discussion. Debatable statements, therefore, have sometimes been purposely included.

T   F   1. The best religion is one that best answers our questions.

T   F   2. If a person seeks affiliation with the church for selfish reasons nothing good can come of it.

T   F   3. People's idea of death is more dreadful than the biblical idea of death.

T   F   4. In the language of Jesus, there are dead people among the living and living ones among the dead.

T   F   5. The words of Jesus, "If you believe in me you shall never die," should not be taken literally.

T   F   6. The basic reason for people's greatest anxieties is a disrupted relationship with God.

T   F   7. Good Christians have no anxieties.

T   F   8. The Bible defines religion as a person's search for God.

T   F   9. It is splitting hair to distinguish between knowing God and knowing about God.

T   F 10. In the language of Jesus, knowing God and having life mean the same thing.

T   F 11. People must acquire the knowledge of God in the same way they acquire all other knowledge.

T   F 12. A person may know the Bible well and not know God.

T   F 13. Christianity is not a reasonable religion because it affirms the limitation and corruption of human reason.

T   F 14. A person could learn from nature, which is God's handiwork, what he or she needs to know about God.

T   F 15. God's word must be something spoken or written down.

T   F 16. In the Bible, God's deeds are God's words.

T   F 17. Christ is called the Word because he taught people the word of God.

T   F 18. Christ participated in the work of creation.

Bible Reading

The concern which prompted you to read this book will, we hope, make you eager to read the Bible. Reading the weekly schedule of Bible readings found at the end of each lesson in this book will contribute greatly to your understanding of the Christian message. Helpful suggestions for reading the Bible are given on page 11, under the heading *Understanding the Bible*.

The Gospel of John
Chapters 1-5

A Prayer for Knowledge

O God, whom to know is life, open our minds and hearts
    to perceive what may be known of you from nature,
    your handiwork, from the happenings in our lives and,
    above all, from your Son, Jesus Christ, your living
    and perfect word.
Grant that our perceiving may be believing, our believing
    trusting and our trusting openness to your love and
    life-giving power; through the same Jesus Christ,
    our Lord.

2

ORDS ABOUT THE
LIVING WORD

PREVIEW

We shall now discuss the following topics: Messengers of God who spoke his word — The word of God meaning the good news of what Christ did for people — The Bible as words about the word of God — The meaning of sacred scriptures being inspired by God — The Bible's human nature — The importance of reading the Bible in the light of its purpose — Difficulties in understanding the Bible — Bible versions — The origin and purpose of creeds — Knowing God as the triune God.

Human Words Are Necessary

In Lesson One we distinguished God's word from human words. Now we need to establish the connection between them. There must be human words to help people recognize the word of God.

The word of God touches people daily but, without being told, they do not acknowledge it. They do not recognize God's voice in nature and in his acts of providence and judgment. They do not respond to the experiences of life by saying, "God has spoken." Except for a few disciples, the people in Palestine in the first century did not know that God was speaking and acting through Christ to bring them salvation and life. Had they known they would not have crucified him. (Luke 22:34; Acts 3:17) The works of God, which are his words, must be proclaimed and explained to people. The message must have messengers. "How are men to call upon him in whom they have not believed? And how are they to believe in him of whom they have not heard? And how are they to hear without a preacher? And how can men preach unless they are sent?" (Romans 10:14-15)

God, whose concern is that people know the life-giving power of his word and believe in him, also provided messengers of his word. The prophets of the Old Testament who explained to people the judgments and gracious acts of God were such messengers. The evangelists and apostles of the New Testament were messengers who told people what God accomplished for them by sending his Son, Christ, into the world.

THE SPOKEN WORD OF GOD

What these messengers of God communicated to people is also called the word of God. The prophets often introduced their message with the words, "Thus says the Lord." Originally they communicated to people through spoken words. Spoken words preceded written words by many years. Old Testament recorded history dates back roughly to 2000 B.C., the time of Abraham. It was not until after 500 B.C. that the Old Testament books, which were really handwritten scrolls, were compiled. The proclamation of the apostles about Jesus were not gathered into a volume until the fourth century. It was not until the invention of the printing press in the fifteenth century that Bible reading began to be common practice among Christians. Yet, in all these virtually Bible-less years, God had his messengers and his people who heeded them.

THE WORD OF GOD AS GOSPEL

In the New Testament "the word of God" becomes "the word of the Lord" and refers specifically to the Gospel, the good news of salvation and life in Jesus Christ. "The living and abiding word of God," Peter says, "is the good news.which was preached to you." (1 Peter 1:23-25) All Christians have been commissioned by their Lord to proclaim the word of God. They do this as often as they tell others what Christ has done for them.

The Bible — The Teaching Word of God

Speaking of the Bible as the written word of God poses some problems. One of them, which has never been solved, is determining which writings should be accepted into the canon, that is, the authoritative list of books that comprise the sacred scriptures. However, neither this problem nor others that will be mentioned later affect the truth that the Bible is the sole source and norm of what Christians today believe and teach. For them it is the teaching word of God.

The Bible is "profitable for teaching, for reproof, for correction, and for training in righteousness, that the man of God may be complete, equipped for every good work." (2 Timothy 3:16-17) To build a house one needs blueprints as well as materials. The Bible provides the blueprints for the making of a complete person of God. By following its directions we become the alive people God would make of us.

WRITTEN BY GOD'S INSPIRATION

The Bible is also the work of God. St. Paul, speaking of the Old Testament, said, "All scripture is inspired by God." (2 Timothy 3:16) *Inspired* means breathed into. These words suggest that just as God breathed into Adam's nostrils the breath of life and he became a living soul (Genesis 2:7), so he breathed life-giving truth into the sacred scriptures. St. Peter wrote, "No prophecy ever came by the impulse of man, but men moved by the Holy Spirit spoke for God." (2 Peter 1:21) The New Testament writers commonly quoted the Old Testament as direct utterances of God. Christ spoke of the words of the prophets as being the word of God and of the Old Testament as "scriptures that cannot be broken" (John 10:35), that "must be fulfilled." (Luke 24:44) He promised his disciples, whose proclamation of the Gospel is preserved for us in the Bible, that his Spirit would guide them into all truth. (John 16:11)

The Bible offers no explanation of how, for the most part, God communicated with those who spoke his word. It is apparent from reading the different books of the Bible that each author thought out his message and wrote in his own style. The dictation theory, which assumes that the writers acted as God's secretaries (today largely displaced by recording machines) was held by rabbis in our Lord's day. It resulted, as we learn from the Gospels, in such a picayune preoccupation with individual words of sacred scriptures that they missed the message, not seeing the forest because of the trees. Similar theories of inspiration have emerged in the Christian church, usually with the same evil results.

Saying that the Bible was inspired by God serves the purpose of establishing its trustworthiness as a book that will lead us to the knowledge of Christ, our Savior. St. Paul said, "All scripture is inspired by God," but only after defining "all scripture" as "sacred writings which are able to instruct you for salvation through faith in Christ Jesus." (2 Timothy 3:15-16) All we know and need to know is that the Bible is a divinely authorized guide to lead us to Christ.

The Bible also has great power: power to teach, reprove, correct and train in righteousness. (2 Timothy 3:16) It is living and active, sharp, piercing and discerning the thoughts and intentions of the heart. (Hebrews 4:12) It is like seed which, when it is received in good soil, produces a harvest of righteousness. (Matthew 13:3-9) The power of the Bible is not a magical power of words. It is the power of Christ, the life-giving word, who is the heart of its message.

"Christ is to the Bible," Luther said, "what the kernel is to the shell, the seed to the pod, the infant to the crib."

THE BIBLE'S HUMAN NATURE

Whereas the dynamic word of God has only a divine nature, the teaching word of God, the Bible, has both a divine and a human nature. God employed human beings, using human language with all of its shortcomings, to speak and write for him. His messengers were all, like us, creatures of their age. They shared the scientific or unscientific views of their generation. Many human factors were involved in gathering, translating and preserving for many centuries, without the benefit of a single original manuscript, the oral and written messages which make up our Bible. The human element also enters into our understanding of the Bible. For example, identifying the different forms of language used in the Bible (narrative, poetic, parabolic, prophetic) sometimes results in differences of opinion. Is this word, or passage or book, to be understood literally or figuratively? In this area Christians will not always be in agreement. One should not expect to have final answers relating to the problems of canonicity, authorship, arrangement of materials, spurious passages, chronology, translation and interpretation. But let's add quickly that these problems never greatly trouble people for whom the Bible has accomplished its purpose of leading them to the knowledge of God and Christ. Their final verdict will be, "One thing I know, that though I was blind, now I see." (John 9:25)

In one way, the Bible is like a telephone book. The telephone book gives you the information you need to communicate with someone you cannot see. A person may say, "How do you know all the information in it is correct? May there not be some wrong numbers?" Your answer would be, "Look, I use it every day. It works. Try it. Besides, there is no other book to take its place." This is the Christian's answer to the person who questions the trustworthiness of the Bible. "It works for me and millions of people. It connects us with Christ. It never fails when you make the right use of it. You had better use it because there is no substitute for it."

READING THE BIBLE IN THE LIGHT OF ITS PURPOSE

The Bible should be read in the light of its purpose. Its sole concern is a right relationship with God and people that it calls life. It bears witness to Christ who offers us eternal life. (John 5:39) It is written "that you may believe that Jesus is the Christ, the Son of God, and that believing you may have life in his name." (John 20:31)

The Bible was not intended to be an encyclopedia with answers for every conceivable question. It is not a textbook on science or a book of moral and civil laws. Quoting the Bible for a purpose alien to its concern commonly results in error and even gross injustice. "The Bible says" has been made the justification for waging unholy wars, the torture of Jews, the persecution of scientists, the enslavement of black people and the subjugation of women. There is no evil that the Bible can not serve when it is not read in the light of its purpose. It is proper to say "The Bible says" only when what follows agrees with what the writers of the Bible were trying to say and accomplish.

UNDERSTANDING THE BIBLE

For the uninitiated, which also describes many Christians, the Bible is a formidable book. Its thought patterns and word meanings are often strange to us. We have already discovered the different meanings that it attaches to such common words as *life, death* and *knowledge*. As we go on we shall see the need of reading new meanings into other simple words if we want to understand the Bible. The trouble lies partly in the difference between our secular and non-godly use of words and the completely God-centered language of the Bible. There, life is not walking and talking; it is walking and talking with God.

Abraham Lincoln mentioned another difficulty when he said, "What troubles me about the Bible is not what I do not understand but what I do understand." Jesus explained the darkness in which people grope when they are confronted by the truths of the Bible by saying, "This is the judgment, that the light has come into the world, and men loved darkness rather than light, because their deeds were evil." (John 3:19) The problem of understanding the Bible is far more moral than intellectual. It requires wanting to understand it, accepting its judgments, taking our thoughts and desires captive to obey Christ. (2 Corinthians 10:5) We must go to it prepared to become what it will make of us. We must take hold of it by letting go of preconceived ideas of religion, prejudices, pet sins and evil habits. The implanted word is able to save our souls when it is received with meekness. (James 1:21) This spirit of letting the word of God shape us, like clay in the potter's hands, is the elementary gift for which we need to pray when we approach the Bible.

The Bible is God's message to us and therefore always relevant and timely. A profitable reading of the Bible requires that we find ourselves in everything we read. We must immediately proceed from the question, "What does this mean?" to "What does this mean to me?" One good way of accomplishing this is by reading a passage or chapter and then asking ourselves three questions: 1) Of what blessings do these words remind me for which I should thank God? 2) Of what sins do they remind me for which I should ask God's forgiveness? 3) Of what duties toward God and people do they remind me for the performance of which I must ask God's help? Thus Bible reading will nourish our life with God.

BIBLE VERSIONS

The Bible, originally written in the Hebrew (Old Testament) and Greek (New Testament) languages has been translated into hundreds of languages and dialects. There are numerous English Bible versions. The King James Version, published in 1611, is still widely used. The biblical quotations in this book are taken from the Revised Standard Bible, published in 1952 for the purpose of giving us a Bible in modern English. Comparing other modern versions (The New English Bible, Good News, [a publication of the American Bible Society], The New Jerusalem Bible) may be very helpful.

Creeds

Creeds (from the Latin word *credo* meaning "I believe") have also helped to preserve the knowledge of the word of God. We have in mind not creeds which characterize one body of Christians in distinction from others (denominational creeds) but ecumenical creeds which sum up vital truths which all Christians hold in common. A common custom among Christians is to confess a creed in their services of worship.

Creeds may also be thought of as weapons, offensive and defensive, with which the church fights to preserve its treasure of faith. The children of God in Old Testament times had their creeds. Surrounded by idolaters who worshipped numerous tribal gods and things that God made instead of God himself, they recited, and taught their children to say, "The Lord our God is one Lord; and you shall love the Lord your God with all your heart, and with all your soul, and with all your might." (Deuteronomy 6:4-5) This formula further distinguished their god from the abstract gods of philosophy. The god who is worshipped and loved is an "I" and not an "it" (nature, law, principle). In their articles of faith they portrayed God as the wholly other, professing his sovereignty and infinity (immeasurableness) by calling him holy, eternal, almight, all-wise, forgiving and gracious. They used different names for God, each with a different shade of meaning for different people and occasions, such as Lord, King, Shepherd and many more.

The Apostles' Creed is the oldest post-biblical creed. Traditional thinking places its origin in apostolic days in connection with the administration of baptism. The candidate for baptism was required to make a confession of his or her Christian faith, and the formula for such a confession may have been the nucleus of this ancient creed. It is so used today. In the course of centuries it was enlarged to its present form.

The Nicene Creed, which adheres to the threefold division of the Apostles' Creed, dates back to the fourth century when a dispute arose about the deity of Christ. It confesses Christ as God, equal in majesty with the Father. Note the emphasis of this truth in the second article (page 133).

The Lutheran Church adopted creeds, or confessions as they are commonly called, which grew out of the 16th century reformation of the church. They are called ecumenical confessions because they profess truths which the reformers believed should be accepted by all Christians. The basic Lutheran confession is the Augsburg Confession (1530) which sought to establish peace and harmony in the church through a consensus on teachings that conform to the Gospel of Jesus Christ. Luther's Small Catechism, found on the last pages of this book, is the most widely known Lutheran confession. It was written as a book of instruction for people, old and young, with limited Christian knowledge.

The Triune God

The term *triune* (three—one) *God* originated in the fourth century in connection with the Nicene Creed which declares Christ to be God without in any way denying that there is but one God. It reduces to a single word the great mystery of the biblical revelation about the three persons of God. The three persons—Father, Son and Holy Spirit—are clearly distinguished in the New Testament. Jesus said, "Go and make disciples of all nations, baptizing them in the name of the Father and of the Son and of the Holy Spirit." (Matthew 28:19) The Father sent his Son into the world. (John 3:16) The Holy Spirit is sent forth from both the Father and the Son. (John 15:26) Each person bears the title of God. Yet, the Bible insists that there is only one God. The trinity in unity, confessed by all Christians, is wholly an article of faith for which no reasonable explanation can be given.

Keeping separate the three persons of the Godhead is the biblical way of making clear to us God's activities in behalf of our salvation. The Father is the creator and author of life. He demonstrated his love for people by giving them his Son. The Son became man to carry out the Father's plan for their lives. The Holy Spirit establishes the vital link of faith between Christ and people. Through the Son we have access in one Spirit to the Father. (Ephesians 2:18) The triune God is the end, means and power of our life. The three articles of the Apostles' Creed and the Nicene Creed present the doctrine of the triune God not as a puzzle to be solved but as a portrayal of the threefold, life-giving activity of God.

Talking It Over

Use each of the following statements as a basis for discussion.

1. —why human words about the word of God are necessary

2. —the priority of spoken messages from God over written messages

3. —the word of God as good news about Christ

4. —the sense in which Christians speak of the Bible as the word of God

5. —what Bible writers being inspired by God means

6. —the purpose that reading the Bible as God-inspired serves

7. —the Bible's human nature

8. —the importance of reading the Bible in the light of its purpose

9. —difficulties in understanding the Bible

10. —Bible versions

11. —the origin and purpose of creeds

12. —the meaning of the term *triune God*

True and False Statements

Circle the letter **T** for true statements and the letter **F** for false statements.

T F 1. No word spoken or written by people should be called the word of God.

T F 2. Reading the Bible has always been the chief source of knowledge for God's people.

T F 3. The good news of what Christ did for us is called the word of God in the New Testament.

T F 4. "The Bible says" should clinch every argument..

T F 5. Since Moses was God's messenger he must have known that his contemporaries were wrong in thinking the world was flat.

T　F　6. Science and the Bible can never be brought into harmony.

T　F　7. It would be ideal if all civil laws were based on the Bible.

T　F　8. Christians treasure the Bible because it leads them to the knowledge of Christ as their Lord and Savior.

T　F　9. Understanding the Bible is not a problem for educated people.

T　F　10. Deeds are more important than creeds.

T　F　11. The Apostles' Creed was written to settle a dispute about Christian doctrine.

T　F　12. The Nicene Creed stresses the equality of Christ with God, the Father.

T　F　13. The Augsburg Confession was written to set Lutherans apart from Roman Catholics.

T　F　14. The term *triune God* is taken from the New Testament.

T　F　15. The three persons of the Godhead are carefully distinguished in the New Testament.

T　F　16. It is not reasonable to believe that there is but one God when there are three distinct persons in the Godhead.

For Further Study

Apply the following three questions to the Bible passages listed below.

- Of what blessings do these words remind me for which I should thank God?

- Of what sins do they remind me for which I should ask God's forgiveness?

- Of what duties do they remind me for the performance of which I must ask God's help?

Psalm 23; Luke 10:25-37; 1 Corinthians 13

Bible Reading

The Gospel of John
Chapters 6-11

A Prayer for a Profitable Reading of the Bible

O Lord,
> your word is before us.
> Grant us a meek and teachable mind while we read
> and study it.
You yourself be our teacher.
> Enlighten our minds and prepare our hearts.
> What we do not see show us, and
> where we are wrong correct us.
Accomplish your purpose of instructing us for salvation
> through Christ Jesus.

3

HE CREATOR OF LIFE

PREVIEW

Our knowledge of God, we have learned, must be derived from God's self-revelation. God made and still makes himself known to people by his work of creation. The Bible begins (Genesis 1 and 2) with this presentation of God as the author of all life, both physical and spiritual.

The topics we shall discuss in this lesson are: The creator our Father — What the biblical stories of creation teach and do not teach — We live in God's world — Adam and Eve, the ideal people of God's creation — What it means to believe in God the Father almighty, maker of heaven and earth.

(See the First Article of the Apostles' Creed and its explanation, page 133.)

Creator and Father

The concept of God in the Bible is overwhelming. In contrast to heathen nations that worshiped tribal gods with limited power and jurisdiction, the God of Israel is the creator of the universe and God of all nations. "O Lord, God of our fathers, art thou not God in heaven? Dost thou not rule over all the kingdoms of the nations? In thy hand are power and might, so that none is able to withstand thee." (2 Chronicles 20:6) In him, whether or not they acknowledge it, people "live and move and have [their] being." (Acts 17:28) He is the author of all life, physical and spiritual. "From him and through him and to him are all things." (Romans 11:36) All things belong to him. "Thine, O Lord, is the greatness, and the power, and the glory, and the victory, and the majesty; for all that is in the heavens and the earth is thine; thine is the kingdom, O Lord, and thou art exalted as head above all." (1 Chronicles 29:11) He has an exclusive claim on every person's life. "The earth is the Lord's and the fulness thereof, the world and those who dwell therein." (Psalm 24:1) Nothing happens without his command or permission. Good and evil (as punishment for sin) proceed from him. "Is it not from the mouth of the Most High that good and evil come? Why should a living man complain, a man, about the punishment of his sins? (Lamentations 3:38-39)

Is not the thought of such a holy, sovereign and inescapable God terrifying? Yes, indeed, unless we can say with the Christian church in the words of the Apostles' Creed, "I believe in God, the Father Almighty, Maker of heaven and earth." To confess God as Father emphasizes the need of standing in a right relationship with him as his children which the Bible calls life. It is frightening for people outside God's family to think of him as "Almighty, Maker of heaven and earth." It is with pride and joy that his children say, "The Lord and maker of the universe is our father," or in the words of Psalm 47:7, "God is the king of all the earth; sing praises with a psalm!"

BIBLICAL STORIES OF CREATION

The first two chapters of Genesis bring together two creation stories. The first (Genesis 1-2:3, where the first chapter should really end) tells the story of the creation of the universe. The second (Genesis 2:4-24) limits itself to the creation of our planet earth. The first uses the name God and the second calls him Lord God suggesting, according to many Christian scholars, different authors.

Christians are not agreed on whether the biblical stories of creation should be read literally as factual prose or as a poetic expression of a child of God's faith. They may be read profitably either way. A literal reading, however, will pose great problems.

In Genesis 1 the primordial element is water which needs to be controlled. In Genesis 2 it is a vast desert which needs to be watered. In Genesis 1 man and woman are created last, after all plants and animals. In Genesis 2 man is created first, before plants and animals, and woman is created last. The method of creation varies in the two stories. In the first, creation is accomplished by God's command, "Let there be." In the second, God is pictured as a sculptor. The verbs are "made," "formed," "took." What is evident from these and other variations is that the authors were not concerned about physical details, which were mere background scenery for their dramas. Different dramas require different settings.

Neither were they concerned about providing us with a textbook on cosmology or astronomy. Nothing is lost in instruction for salvation, which was their sole concern, by acknowledging the primitiveness of their scientific knowledge. Let Copernicus be the founder of astronomy. They were inspired to be the founders of theology. Let science pursue its study of the mechanics of the universe. Let the church worship the creator who rules over it and makes it work.

At the beginning of all things (light, day and night, the heavens and the earth, people, marriage, procreation, freedom to choose between good and evil), stands the preexistent God. "In the beginning God...." (Genesis 1:1) Things come into being by his mere word of command. The description befits the majesty of God. The only proper response is, "O come, let us worship and bow down, let us kneel before the Lord, our Maker!" (Psalm 95:6) Or, as in the second story, he is the God who puts himself into his creation, the sculptor who fashions man and woman with loving hands and the gardener who stoops to plant trees and flowers for their enjoyment. It is the picture of a God whose "compassion is over all that he has made." (Psalm 145:9)

THE PURPOSE OF THE CREATION STORIES

The purpose of the biblical creation stories is the worship and adoration of God. They establish God's lordship over the universe and the creator—creature relationship between God and people. "Know that the Lord is God! It is he that made us, and we are his; we are his people, and the sheep of his pasture." (Psalm 100:3) A day of worship is even ordained. (Genesis 2:2-3) Here is the biblical concern about the knowledge of God which is life.

The Bible gives the right answers when we ask the right questions. The right questions about the biblical stories of creation relate to the acknowledgment of God as creator and life-giver. We look in vain here for answers to questions that science may raise about the age of the earth and evolutionary processes. Nothing matters but this: "Know that the Lord is God" of the universe, of nature and its laws, of our world and our lives. God's words, "Let there be," is the final explanation for every birth and for all the processes of procreation and reproduction. This is implied in the words "seed" (Genesis 1:11-12) and "be fruitful and multiply." (Genesis 1:22, 28) We live in God's world, teeming with life with which he continually renews the face of the earth. "When thou takest away their breath, they die and return to their dust. When thou sendest forth the Spirit, they are created; and thou renewest the face of the ground." (Psalm 104:29-30)

Finally, it is the creation and providence of God that surround us that should lead us to worship God. It is seeing ourselves as Adam or Eve that prompts us to acknowledge him. Observe that Luther's explanation of the first article of the Apostles' Creed is a personal confession, beginning with the words, "I believe that God has created me," and ending with the words, "Therefore I surely ought to thank and praise, serve and obey him."

The First People

Adam and Eve are by far the most important creatures of Genesis 1 and 2. They are living people. God brings them not only into existence but into a wonderful relationship with himself. He crowns them with honor and glory. (Psalm 8:5) He forms their bodies with his own hands. He speaks with them and gives them the faculty to receive his word, obey it and to communicate with him. He blesses them and gives them dominion over all created things. The world was made for them. They have license to explore and use for their benefit whatever they find in it. There is God-given sanction here for all the sciences in the measure that they contribute to God's glory and the well-being of people. They have freedom of choice, power and responsibility, under God, of course. Of particular significance is the statement (Genesis 1:27) that God created them in his own image. They bear a likeness to God. As true children they resemble their glorious father. They reflect his righteousness. As is true of no other creature, they acknowledge God and live in conscious communion with him.

ADAM AND EVE, THE IDEAL PEOPLE

We have been speaking of human beings' honor and glory in the present tense to indicate what God's high intentions still are for all people. Here is God's goal for people which the first two chapters of the Bible help us to realize. The "very good" Adam and Eve are the alive persons God would have us all be. The creation stories, furthermore, assure us that God has power to bring into being people who enjoy the fulness of life. They offer the hope of our becoming the Adam and Eve of Genesis. How God accomplishes this is what the rest of the Bible goes on to relate.

Of course, we can not ignore the fact that the creation stories of Genesis are written in the past tense. They are written in the knowledge that their picture of people is no longer true. A later story (Genesis 3) will relate what Adam and Eve, who portray us, did with their freedom and responsibility, their power and glory. This sad story, however, does not belong in the account of creation, which is the work of God unsullied by sin. The Adam and Eve of Genesis 1 and 2 are the kind of people he creates and for whom he takes responsibility. They are very good people because whatever he creates is very good. Evil is never of his making. "Every good endowment and every perfect gift is from above, coming down from the Father of lights with whom there is no variation or shadow due to change." (James 1:17)

Faith in God, the Creator

The creator God, as close to us as everything we touch, is the God in whom we must believe. The church teaches us to say, "I believe in God, the Father Almighty, Maker of heaven and earth." With this confession we are accounting for our lives, our world, our health and powers, our sustenance, our homes and families, our daily work.

What does it mean to say, "I believe in God"? Here again, common usage of a word will lead us astray. Many Americans would say, "I believe in God." By this they probably mean no more than that they believe there is a God. Such a faith is simply giving mental consent to a proposition, like saying, "I believe in the law of gravity." It does not lead to saying, "therefore I ought to thank and praise, serve and obey him."

FAITH—A RELATIONSHIP WORD

A Christian does not only say "I believe that" but also "I believe in." Believing in God means standing in an intimate relationship with God. Believing in God, knowing God and having life finally mean the same thing in the Bible.

FAITH AS TRUST

Faith in God is not merely acknowledging God's existence, or giving mental consent to numerous propositions about God. This may be a devilish thing. "You believe that God is one; you do well. Even the demons believe—and shudder." (James 2:19) Faith traces all blessings back to God. It is trust and reliance on the goodness and life-giving power of God.

BELIEVING IS SEEING

It is often said that seeing is believ ng. The Bible reverses this and says believing is seeing. "Faith... is the conviction of things not seen." (Hebrews 11:1) It is only by faith that God can be known. In one sense, he is the Father almighty, maker of heaven and earth only to the person who believes him to be this. Faith in God involves a risk. The only way to certainty is by daring to believe.

FAITH LETS GOD BE GOD

"Faith," Luther said, "is the highest worship, the greatest obedience, the most pleasing sacrifice that can be offered to God. A person never has anything better to give God than glory. Faith gives God glory." It honors God for what he is. It lets God be God.

FAITH ACCEPTS WHAT GOD OFFERS

Faith is openness. It is the hand which a person opens and extends to receive from God what he has to offer. It accepts God's gifts, above all, his gift of life. Jesus would say to people who wanted his help that what they believed he would do for them is precisely what would be done for them. "According to your faith be it done to you." (Matthew 9:29) People see as much of God and experience as much of his power as their faith permits. They meet the problems of life with the stunted God of their faith. This explains why the admonition to believe in God occurs far more frequently in the Bible than any other.

THE BELIEVER AS GOD'S CREATION

What we previously said about life and knowledge must also be said about faith. It, too, is a gift of God and not a human accomplishment. Adam and Eve, the believers in God, are God's creation.

FAITH VITALLY AFFECTS OUR LIFE

The words, "I believe in God, the Father Almighty, Maker of heaven and earth," spoken by Christians in their services of worship and prayers, are not meant to be a shibboleth or ritualistic formula. They are a way of life. They bring God into our plans, our work, our joys and sorrows, our hopes and fears. We are "the sheep of his pasture." (Psalm 100:3) Our times are in his hands. (Psalm 31:15) Without his blessing our labor is in vain. (Psalm 127:1)

Faith in God as creator and provider drives out of our hearts fear, worry and anxiety. It rules out greed and covetousness and being oversensitive about what people think of us. It engenders courage and confidence, peace of mind, sleepful nights and thankfulness.

"Do not be anxious, saying 'What shall we eat?' or 'What shall we drink?' or 'What shall we wear?'... Your heavenly Father knows that you need them all." (Matthew 6:31-32)

"If I have rejoiced because my wealth was great, or because my hand had gotten much... I should have been false to God above." (Job 31:25-28)

"We can confidently say, 'The Lord is my helper, I will not be afraid; what can a man do to me?'" (Hebrews 13:6)

"Wait for the Lord; be strong, and let your heart take courage." (Psalm 27:14)

"Thou dost keep them in perfect peace, whose mind is stayed on thee, because he trusts in thee." (Isaiah 26:3)

"If you sit down, you will not be afraid; when you lie down, your sleep will be sweet... for the Lord will be your confidence." (Proverbs 3:24-26)

"Always and for everything giving thanks in the name of our Lord Jesus Christ to God the Father." (Ephesians 5:20)

Talking It Over

Use each of the following statements and question as a basis for discussion.

1. How does the God of the Bible differ from heathen gods?

2. —the need of knowing the almighty God as our Father

3. —the differences in the two creation stories and why they should not disturb us

4. —the purpose of the Genesis stories of creation

5. —the importance of recognizing God as our creator

6. —the evidences of Adam and Eve being alive persons in the biblical sense

7. —our interest in Adam and Eve as the ideal persons of God's creation

8. —what people commonly mean and what the Bible means by believing in God

9. —the relationship between faith, knowledge and life

10. —how faith in God relates to our daily life

True and False Statements

Circle the letter **T** for true statements and the letter **F** for false statements.

T F   1. It might be terrifying simply to say, "I believe in God Almighty."

T F   2. The differences between the two creation stories in Genesis must be regarded by Christians as a worrisome problem.

T F   3. If the biblical creation stories lead us to worship God as creator and life-giver their purpose has been accomplished.

T F   4. The Bible is the world's best textbook on science.

T F   5. Creation is pictured as a finished work in Genesis 1 and 2.

T F   6. We worship God not because of a world he created ages ago but because all our present blessings come from him.

T F   7. Genesis 1 and 2 speak primarily of the creation of physical life and material things.

T   F   8. The Bible rules out the thought of the earth being millions of years old.

T   F   9. Whether or not one gets the message of Genesis 1 and 2 depends on whether one reads it as a narrative of what happened or as a poetic expression of a child of God's faith.

T   F   10. Adam and Eve are the ideal persons that God would have everyone be.

T   F   11. There is no hope that anyone could ever become the Adam and Eve of Genesis.

T   (F) 12. Adam and Eve's "image of God" means they once looked like God.

T   F   13. People readily understand what the Bible means by believing in God.

T   F   14. When our faith in God is limited, God's power that we experience is also limited.

T   F   15. The Bible teaches that believing is seeing.

T   F   16. The person who believes in God is always on right terms with God.

T   F   17. Faith, knowledge and life often mean the same thing in the Bible.

T   F   18. Believing in God frees a person from all anxieties.

T   F   19. Faith in God is a real solution to our biggest problems.

T   F   20. Faith in God assures us of success in all of our undertakings.

Bible Reading

The Book of Genesis
Chapters 1-2 and 12-16

The Book of Psalms
Psalm 104

A Prayer for Joy in God's Creation

O heavenly Father,
who has filled the world with beauty,
open our eyes to behold your gracious hand
in all works,
so that we may rejoice in your whole creation
and serve you with gladness,
for the sake of our Lord Jesus Christ,
through whom all things were made.

4

HE LOSS OF LIFE

PREVIEW

There is a wide difference between the very good world of God's creation and the world in which we live. The difference is between life and death. We have not fallen heir to the blessedness of Adam and Eve's life with and under God. God's ideal persons were not reproduced. What happened? Who is to blame for sin and death? Not God, but people. It is vitally important for people to recognize and confess their guilt and helplessness. They are not willing, of their own accord, to do this. But God, who never gives up on his dreams and plans for people, offers his help.

In this lesson we shall discuss the biblical story of how people lost the supreme gift of life — good and evil spirits — the nature of sin and sinful human nature — the result of sin — people's helplessness — the importance and difficulty of confessing sins — the help God offers — confessing sins to one another — confessing to the pastor.

The Fall

Genesis 1 and 2 pictures people not as they are but as God would have them be. The people we know do not live in blissful communion with God. They do not use their gifts and powers to the glory of God and their own best interests. They are destroyers whose growing scientific knowledge is a growing threat to the world God created. They violate God's institutions of worship, labor and marriage, and have turned the garden of Eden into a valley of tears.

Genesis 3 describes, in the language of the church, humankind's fall. It tells how Adam and Eve disobeyed God. The penalty was death. God warned Adam about the forbidden tree of which he ate, saying, "The day you eat of it you shall die." (Genesis 2:17) He and Eve ate of it and died, not just physically years later, but immediately in the biblical sense. Overcome by a sense of guilt and shame they tried to hide. They sought existence apart from God. The story teaches the universal truth that "the wages of sin is death." (Romans 6:23)

The reason for their disobedience was doubt about God's concern for their well-being. The story pictures people asking, "Do I really fare best when I submit to the rule of God's word? Is not God's rule over one's life a restriction of one's freedom to achieve happiness and power?" These are the questions involved in every act of disobedience to God. Sin is always people wanting to go their own way. This further implies wanting to be like God (Genesis 3:3), because they presume to have the right to do as they please rather than what pleases God. This is the "way which seems right to a man, but its end is the way of death." (Proverbs 14:12)

Angels

Genesis 3 introduces the realm of angels, specifically a fallen angel. The wily serpent that beguiled Eve is later identified in the Bible as being the devil. (1 John 3:8) Philosophical questions about the origin of evil are left unanswered in Genesis 3. Suddenly and without explanation an evil spirit appears on the scene. Where does he come from? One thing is certain. God, from whom all good and only good comes, did not create anything evil. The evil spirits are spoken of in the Bible as angels who did not keep their position (Jude, v.6) but sinned and were cast into hell. (2 Peter 2:4)

GOOD ANGELS

Angels are not mentioned in Genesis 1 and 2. Their existence is accepted on the basis of many other biblical passages. They are especially prominent in the major events of Christ's earthly life (his birth, Luke 1:26-28; 2:8-15; his suffering in Gethsemane, Luke 22:43; his resurrection from death, Matthew 28:5-7). They are spirits who sometimes assumed a human form. They are holy (Mark 8:38), of great number (Luke 2:13), and powerful. (Psalm 103:20) They serve as God's messengers to people, as in the Christmas and Easter stories. They praise God and carry out his commands, relating especially to the safety and well-being of his people. The thought of children having guardian angels is based on the saying of Christ (Matthew 18:10) in which he speaks of "their angels" to show how much God cares for and about them. The words "little ones" in this passage embraces all who are little according to worldly standards of greatness.

FALLEN ANGELS

The Bible has much to say about the power and work of fallen angels. They are called devils, which means adversaries. They are enemies of both God and people. The prince of devils is called Satan, which means accuser. He delights in plaguing a person's conscience with feelings of guilt. He commands a host of evil spirits (Mark 5:9), is cunning (Genesis 3:1), and powerfully influential and effective. (Ephesians 6:12) He tempts people to sin and afflicts them physically, mentally and emotionally. (Luke 13:16; 2 Corinthians 12:7) In short, he strives with phenomenal success to drag people down to his own misery, and to destroy God's creation. Since we are victimized by Satan it was necessary for our Savior to conquer him by overcoming Satan's temptations. (Matthew 4:1-11)

Some obvious and inescapable truths are implied in the biblical doctrine of evil spirits. A person's soul or personality is open to invasion by evil forces from the outside. We find with St. Paul that we cannot control or even understand our own actions. Often we do not do what we want to do but the very thing we hate. (Romans 7:15) We find ourselves contending with a power that we acknowledge to be both alien and tyrannical. People often say, "I don't know what possessed me." The Bible sometimes calls the alien spirit the devil. We are not merely contending against flesh and blood, St. Paul says, but against the powers in control, the rulers of darkness (Ephesians 6:12), "the father of lies," Jesus says (John 8:44), the hateful spirit that dictates hateful words and deeds. Satan is the tenant who occupies a person's house and must be driven out. (Luke 11:21-26)

Evidences of demonic possession are as plentiful in our scientific age as in the days of our Lord. In view of the holocaust of Nazi concentration camps in World War II, the psychoanalyst Jung returned to the biblical doctrine of demons.

What God accomplished through Christ's redemptive work St. Paul summed up in the words, "He delivered us from the dominion of darkness and transferred us to the kingdom of his Son." (Colossians 1:13)

Acknowledging the existence of an alien, tyrannical spirit, or spirits, does not absolve a person from blame and guilt. It was in vain that Eve offered the excuse, "The serpent beguiled me, and I ate." (Genesis 3:13) There is a close affinity between the temptations of the devil and people's desires, which explains the devil's success. People are tempted when they are lured and enticed by their own desire. "Then desire when it has conceived gives birth to sin; and sin when it is full-grown brings forth death." (James 1:14-15)

The Nature of Sin

Sin means missing the mark of perfection which God has set up for us. Other names for sin are: disobedience (Romans 5:19); debt (Matthew 6:12); lawlessness (1 John 3:4); iniquity (unequity, uneveness) (Exodus 34:7); fault (Matthew 18:15); trespass (2 Corinthians 5:19); wickedness (Romans 6:13); wrong (Colossians 3:25); rebellion (Isaiah 30:1).

There are sins of thought, word and deed. There are sins of commission (doing wrong) and sins of omission (failing to do what should be done). Sin corrupts a person's feelings and attitudes. "The works of the flesh are plain: fornication, impurity, licentiousness, idolatry, sorcery, enmity, strife, jealousy, anger, selfishness, dissension, party spirit, envy, drunkenness, carousing, and the like." (Galatians 5:19-21) People often conceal their hateful feelings beneath an outward veneer of polite words and proper deeds. "Like the glaze covering an earthen vessel are smooth lips with an evil heart." (Proverbs 26:23)

Society classifies sins in terms of crimes, misdemeanors, petty offenses and numerous wrongs that it winks at. Classifying sins often results in regarding the sins of others as being the big ones and one's own as being little. The Bible does, however, distinguish between deliberate and unintentional sins, sinning against knowledge or in ignorance. "That servant who knew his master's will, but did not make ready or act according to his will, shall receive a severe beating. But he who did not know, and did what deserved a beating, shall receive a light beating." (Luke 12:47-48) Every sin pushes God away, questions or denies his claim upon us and lordship over us.

SINFUL HUMAN NATURE

The word *sin* does not just describe a wrong word, feeling or action. It describes a person's original state of separation from God, being dead through sins. St. Paul said of some new Christians, "You he made alive, when you were dead through the trespasses and sins in which you once walked." (Ephesians 2:1) This death is further described as hostility toward God which incurs his wrath. "The wrath of God is revealed from heaven against all ungodliness and wickedness of men." (Romans 1:18)

People are by nature sinful. They do not acquire sinfulness after they are born. They are born sinners. This is what our Lord meant when he said, "That which is born of the flesh is flesh." (John 3:6) Sinners beget sinners as naturally as apple trees bear apples. Because all creatures clothed with human flesh are sinners, flesh and sinfulness often mean the same thing in the New Testament. "If you doubt your sinfulness," Luther said, "just pinch yourself and notice what you are holding between your fingers." This is not registering disgust with the human body, but with what sin can make of it.

ORIGINAL SIN

The Church describes a person's sinful nature as original or inherited sin. Its origin can be traced back to our first parents. It is an inheritance which is passed on from one generation to another. As an old couplet puts it: "In Adam's fall—We sinned all." For all practical purposes, Adam acted as humankind's representative when he sinned, just as Christ acted as humankind's representative when he conquered sin. "If many died through one man's trespass, much more have the grace of God and the free gift in the grace of that one man Jesus Christ abounded for many." (Romans 5:15) Original sin means a person is spiritually stillborn. Born in sin describes people's plight in the face of their religious problem of getting on right terms with God. They are born outside the kingdom of God and need a rebirth fathered by the Holy Spirit to enter the kingdom of God. Jesus said, "Truly, truly, I say to you, unless one is born anew, he cannot see the kingdom of God." (John 3:3)

HOW MUCH HELP DO WE NEED?

The biblical doctrine of original sin runs against the grain of American self-confidence and optimism. Yet, as C.S. Lewis said, it is a doctrine which, unlike most others, can be verified by observation. More importantly, it is essential to the good news about a God who brings life out of death. It relates to what we believe about ourselves. What we believe about ourselves will finally determine the nature and amount of help we shall seek from God. People might believe one of three things about themselves. (1) They might regard themselves as being spiritually healthy and boast about their many good deeds. Christ said of such self-righteous people that they have no need of a physician. God's offer of forgiveness and help does not interest them. (2) People commonly regard themselves as being alternately healthy and sick. They need God occasionally, as they need their doctor. As a rule, they can manage quite well without him. (3) The Christian humbly accepts the Bible's verdict that people, by nature, are dead through sin. This does not mean that their case is hopeless. It means people must rely on God's creative, life-giving power. What needs to be done for them is described as a resurrection. St. Paul said of his new Christians, "You he made alive, when you were dead." (Ephesians 2:1) When we have made up our minds about the meaning of original sin we have gone a long way toward answering the question, "What must God do for me?" We are determining whether we need no God, a doctor God or the God of Genesis who brings people to life.

NO EXCUSE

If the work of the devil does not absolve people from guilt neither does the fact that they are born with a sinful nature. They are not wholly the victims of circumstances. Sinning is always a matter of choice. Very near to forbidden trees of which they eat are good trees which God planted for their enjoyment. The sins which testify against us are always our own sins.

THE TRAGIC RESULTS OF SIN

We experience the tragic results of sin in our body (sickness, death), in our minds (fear, worry), and in our relationships with other people (hatred, strife, warfare). Adam and Eve in their fallen state indulged in hateful incrimination and recrimination. (Genesis 3:12-13) A further picture of suffering and misery resulting from sin is given in Genesis 3:14-19. To this we must add humankind's abuse of nature: the suicidal pollution of the air we breathe, the water we drink and the land we farm.

People should know from bitter experience the dreadfully destructive power of sin. What they fail to realize is that it destroys everything because it destroys their relationship to God. All human misery is comprehended in the statement, "The wages of sin is death,"—separation from God. (Romans 6:23)

To say that all human misery is the result of sin does not, however, warrant the judgment that the more trouble a person has the more sinful he or she must be. The Lord chastises those whom he loves. (Hebrews 12:5-6) Christians are told that they must enter the kingdom of God through much tribulation. (Acts 14:22)

HELL

The never-ending state of death is sometimes called hell. Jesus said, "Do not fear those who kill the body but cannot kill the soul; rather fear him who can destroy both body and soul in hell." (Matthew 10:28) Hell was neither invented by people nor created by God. It is the logical result of human sinfulness. It owes its origin to the obvious truth that a holy God cannot live with people in their state of sinfulness. Nothing remains for God to say to people who delight in godlessness but "Depart from me." (Matthew 25:41)

HUMAN HELPLESSNESS

The word *death* as a description of people's plight emphasizes their utter helplessness to do anything to remove their sin and guilt and God's sentence of damnation. They cannot, as they like to believe, atone for their sins by their "good deeds" or sacrifices. The scriptural terms for this truth are "salvation is not of works" and "salvation is not by the law." This is strongly emphasized in the writings of St. Paul. "No human being will be justified in his sight by works of the law." (Romans 3:20) "All who rely on works of the law are under a curse; for it is written, 'Cursed be every one who does not abide by all things written in the book of the law, and do them.'" (Galatians 3:10) The Bible rules out all "do-it-yourself" religions. Being dead in sin there is nothing a person can do.

God Comes to the Rescue

At this point the life-giving God must be brought into the picture. The Creator is also the God of all mercy, as the story in Genesis 3 reveals. The sinners, Adam and Eve, did not search for God hoping for forgiveness and reconciliation but God searched for and found them. They had no hopes about their future but God still had his dreams and plans for them. There is no sense of hopelessness with him. He is Creator and Life-giver. "He gives life to the dead and calls into existence the things that do not exist." (Romans 4:17) It is a case of the living one meeting with the dead and the first action, naturally, is on the part of the living one.

CONFESSION, THE FIRST STEP

Life with God begins with the sense of need for God's help because of our sinfulness. We are reminded of this in the church service which often begins with a confession of sins. God wants to help us realize our need for forgiveness. He cornered Adam and Eve and sought to wrest a confession from them so that he might forgive them. He let them know that he knew what they had done, saying, "Have you eaten of the tree of which I commanded you not to eat?" (Genesis 3:11) An honest answer would have been the opening of their hearts to receive his forgiveness. "If we confess our sins, he is faithful and just, and will forgive our sins and cleanse from all unrighteousness. If we say we have not sinned, we make him a liar, and his word is not in us." (1 John 1:9-10) Without forgiveness, life with God is not possible. His forgiveness, dependent on our confession, is the removal of sin which separates us from God. "Where there is forgiveness of sins," Luther said, "there is life and salvation."

The Bible expresses this truth in still another way. A person enters into the kingdom of God (enjoys God's rule over his life) by way of repentance. "Repent, for the kingdom of heaven is at hand." (Matthew 3:2) Repentance, in its full sense, embraces three things: (1) making an honest confession of one's sins, (2) being confident of God's forgiveness, (3) forsaking old sins and entering upon a new life of Christlikeness with the help of God. Christian repentance, as we shall later see, grows out of faith in Christ, "who was put to death for our trespasses and raised for our justification." (Romans 4:25) Justification here, as elsewhere in the Bible, is God's act of setting us right with him.

HOW HARD IT IS TO CONFESS

From one point of view, confessing one's sins might seem to be a simple matter. After all, God requires only that we be honest with him and ourselves. In reality, people find it a difficult or even impossible thing to do. Stricken with guilt, Adam and Eve tried to hide from God. When God finally confronted them with their sin they offered excuses and blamed others. This is typical human behavior, as we know from experience. God must corner people, as he did with Adam and Eve, and coax a confession out of them.

Worse even than not confessing their guilt, sinful people delight in boasting about their "goodness." The spirit of self-righteousness is the most deadly sin because it implies the refusal of God's offer of help. To the self-righteous Pharisees of his day, Jesus sarcastically said, "Those who are well have no need of a physician, but those who are sick.... I came not to call the righteous, but sinners." (Matthew 9:12-13) A doctor cannot help a patient with a sore foot if the patient will not remove his or her shoe. Similarly, the heavenly physician has no cure for people who boast in the soundness of their spiritual health and refuse to lay bare their sins.

GOD'S CALL TO REPENT

God strives to lead people to repentance by his word of judgment and condemnation

(God's law). "Through the law comes knowledge of sin." (Romans 3:20) He also does it by visiting people with affliction. God would have the afflicted say, "Come, let us return to the Lord; for he has torn, that he may heal us; he has stricken, and he will bind us up." (Hosea 6:1) Human freedom includes the frightening freedom of being able to say no to God. Luther said, "God does not drag people into heaven by the hair." But when people do not choose to ignore God's call to repent, it has power to raise them from the death of sin to a life of righteousness.

REPENTANCE IS LIFELONG

The life of righteousness to which God calls the believer is always far from being perfect. All Christians must say with St. Paul, "Not that I am already perfect; but I press on... toward the goal for the prize of the upward call of God in Christ Jesus." (Philippians 3:12-14) Repentance is a lifelong practice of every child of God. We must repent daily because we sin daily. Nothing, in fact, distinguishes Christians more clearly than their daily acts of repentance. The closer they walk with God the greater will be their concern to do his will and the more sensitive they will be to sin. But the greater, too, will be their joy in the good news of God's forgiveness. Repentance is the process of growing in Christlikeness.

CONFESSION MUST BE MADE TO GOD

Confession must be made to God because sin is always the transgression of God's law. Christians are sorry for their sins, not because they "made a mess of things," or brought misery upon themselves, but because their sins distress and dishonor their heavenly Father. When no evil consequences follow immediately it is easy to break laws without any feeling of regret. "So I broke a traffic law, but I wasn't caught." It is a different matter when the violation of the law hurts someone who loves us and whom we love. This is the nature of true penitence in the Bible. The psalmist expresses it in the words, "Against thee, thee only, have I sinned, and done that which is evil in thy sight." (Psalm 51:4) The prodigal son, in Christ's parable, expressed his penitence in the words, "Father, I have sinned against heaven and before you; I am no longer worthy to be called your son." (Luke 15:21)

Before God we are bound to confess all our sins, even those of which we may not be aware, as in the "Our Father" and in the service of public worship.

CONFESSING SINS TO ONE ANOTHER

The Bible also requires that Christians confess their sins to people whom they have offended, seeking forgiveness and reconciliation. "Confess your sins to one another, and pray for one another, that you may be healed." (James 5:16) Confession of sins and forgiveness are not only indispensable for life with God but also for living in harmony with people which life with God requires. "If you are offering your gift at the altar, and there remember that your brother has something against you, leave your gift there before the altar and go; first be reconciled to your brother, and then come and offer your gift." (Matthew 5:23-24)

PRIVATE CONFESSION

Christians sometimes confess their sins to other Christians not only to beg pardon but to be assured by them of God's forgiveness. Most commonly such private confession, as it is called, is made to pastors because of their office as shepherds of the flock. Feelings of guilt and a bad conscience, which often afflict Christians, too, can be effectively dealt with in private confession.

What Luther's Small Catechism teaches about private confession will be found on pages 131-139.

Talking It Over

Use each of the following statements and questions as a basis for discussion.

1. —how Genesis 3 describes what death through sin means

2. —what the Bible says about angels

3. —what it says about evil spirits—their origin, work and power

4. Can people today reasonably believe in devils?

5. What is meant by original sin? How does it relate to what we believe God must do for us?

6. What are the results of sin—physically, mentally, socially? What is the worst result?

7. Can we conclude that the more trouble a person has the more sinful he or she must be?

8. Why does the Bible rule out "do-it-yourself" religions?

9. —the importance of confessing sins for a life with God

10. —the biblical meaning of repentance

11. —the difficulty of confessing sins

12. —the need for daily and lifelong repentance

13. —the importance of confession and forgiveness for harmony among people

14. —the good of privately confessing sins to the pastor

True and False Statements

Circle the letter **T** for true statements and the letter **F** for false statements.

T F 1. Nothing of the Adam and Eve in Genesis can be seen in people today.

T F 2. Adam and Eve sinned and really died immediately.

T F 3. The creation stories in Genesis do not mention angels.

T F   4. Angels are superhuman beings who serve God and people.

T F   5. Devils are angels who rebelled against God.

T F   6. A bad conscience is the work of the devil.

T F   7. The devil is responsible for all the evil in the world.

T F   8. Some sins are more damnable than others.

T F   9. Born in sin simply means starting out in life prone to do wrong things.

T F 10. Babies arrive in the world sinless but later learn sin from others.

T F 11. The state of sinfulness is fully described by saying it is doing wrong or not doing what is right.

T F 12. One cannot believe both in a hell and a God of all love.

T F 13. God does not help people to confess their sins.

T F 14. Afflictions should be regarded both as evidences of our sinfulness and of God's love for us.

T F 15. The reason God forgives people is because they humbly confess their sins.

T F 16. God's forgiveness is the promise of a trouble-free and prosperous life.

T F 17. Repentance may be defined as "turning over a new leaf."

T F 18. The most hopeless of all sins is self-righteousness.

T F 19. When God calls people to repent they are bound to do so.

T F 20. People who do not love God may feel very sorry for their sins.

T F 21. We never need to confess our sins to anyone but God.

T F 22. The Lutheran Church encourages its members to make a private confession of sins to the pastor.

Bible Reading

The Book of Genesis
Chapters 3-4 and 17-24

A Prayer for Penitence

Merciful Father,
>   give us grace
>   that we may never presume
>   to sin;
>   but if at any time
>   we offend you,
>   may we truly repent
>   and by a lively faith
>   obtain forgiveness of all our sins,
>   solely through the merits of
>   your Son,
>   our Savior Jesus Christ.

5

CHRIST, OUR LIFE...

PREVIEW

In this chapter we shall discuss the person and work of Christ. We shall see that he was and is just the right person for the work that needed to be done to establish the kingdom of God among people. We shall see that he was and had to be both God and man to keep the law perfectly as humankind's representative and to offer an effective sacrifice for their sins. We shall see how he has performed his office as our prophet, our priest, and our king.

From the Old to the New Testament

The hope of people rests in the God who is pictured to us in the first three chapters of Genesis. He has power to create life and he searches for people to restore them to life. However hopeless and helpless their plight is, the Giver of life is willing and able to come to their rescue.

THE CREATION OF GOD'S PEOPLE

The Old Testament goes on to relate how God brought into being a people who lived under his rule. The story begins with Abraham who received God's promise that he would be the father of a great nation that would be blessed by him and, in turn, would be a blessing to all people. (Genesis 12:2) This nation, truly under God, came into being at the time of Moses. By miraculously rescuing the Israelites from their bondage in Egypt, God made himself known to them as one whose power to deliver people from evil was limitless. He then claimed the rescued Israelites as his people who owed him their loyalty. At Mt. Sinai he gave them his law which bound them fast to him as their benevolent and almighty King. (Exodus 20)

From this story the Old Testament derives its name. Testament means covenant and refers to the wonderful "bargain" which God made with the Israelites when he said, "I will take you for my people, and I will be your God; and you shall know that I am the Lord your God." (Exodus 6:7)

Numerous warranted and unwarranted hopes developed from this covenant relationship: God's protection and help in times of trouble, military victories, the possession of a promised land, sovereignty as a nation, prosperity, and religious liberty.

Under King David these hopes were most fully realized. But these good days were short-lived because of the rebelliousness of the people who failed to keep their part of the covenant. Throughout the Old Testament the tension mounts between God's faithfulness to his promises and the unfaithfulness of his chosen people which compelled God to punish them. Threats of punishment and promises of deliverance intermingle in the message of the prophets. God seemed to be caught in the dilemma of either winking at sin or abandoning his promises.

THE COMING OF THE PROMISED MESSIAH

In the midst of this unresolved issue some new and more glorious promises of God were proclaimed by the prophets. The foremost related to the coming of a messiah, through whom God would make a new covenant with his people to replace the old one which they had broken. His law would be written upon their hearts and they would know and serve him as their loving and forgiving God. (Jeremiah 31:33-34) *Messiah*, or Christ in the Greek language, means the anointed one. In Old Testament times, kings and high priests were anointed as a sign that God had appointed them to their office and granted them an outpouring of his Spirit.

Misconceptions about the office and work of the Messiah abounded among the Israelites. We have the benefit of hindsight. What God intended him to be we can best learn from what in fact he was and is. The message of the New Testament is, Christ has come and is here. He is Jesus of Nazareth whose life and works reveal that he was filled with the Spirit of God. All God's promises are realized in him. God gave him the name Jesus because he came to save his people from their sins. (Matthew 1:21) The people of God and children of Abraham are now all people who believe in him and submit to his rule.

In the language of the New Testament all prophecy was fulfilled in Christ, which means that every bud of hope found in the Old Testament blossoms into a full flower in the person and work of Christ. In him, God's hopes and dreams for people may be fully realized. Believers in Christ are God's new creation, the Adam or Eve of his making who live in his kingdom. The picture will be complete when the new Adams and Eves walk with God in the new paradise of heaven.

The New Testament message is summed up in Luther's explanation of the second article of the Apostles' Creed (page 133).

The Person of Christ

The New Testament, like the Old Testament, begins with a narrative of a person who enjoyed the fullness of life. St. John, in his gospel (John 1:4), says simply, "In him [Christ] was life."

But he was a far greater Adam. God created the first Adam in his image. The artist gave his subject some resemblance to himself. But there is a vast difference between the artist and his handiwork, between the creator and the creature. The failure of people to acknowledge this difference, according to Genesis (Gen. 3:5), is the root of all sin.

TRUE GOD

Unlike the first Adam, Christ was not merely created in God's image. He was and is the Son of God who inherited the nature of God. "Like father, like son" was literally true in his case. What is blasphemous for God's creature to say, namely, "I and the Father are one," he could and did say. (John 10:30) "In him the whole fullness of deity dwells bodily." (Colossians 2:9) "He reflects the glory of God and bears the very stamp of his nature." (Hebrew 1:3)

In him "are hid all the treasures of wisdom and knowledge." (Colossians 2:3) All authority in heaven and on earth were given to him (Matthew 28:18). He insisted on being honored as God, saying, "He who does not honor the Son does not honor the Father who sent him." (John 5:23) He upholds the universe by his word of power. (Hebrews 1:3) He claimed the power to forgive sins, saying, "The Son of Man has authority on earth to forgive sins." (Matthew 9:6) The Father has given him authority to execute judgment. (John 5:27) He performed many miracles by his own power and in his own name including, as his crowning miracle, his rising from death. He was "designated Son of God in power according to the Spirit of holiness by his resurrection from the dead." (Romans 1:4) He is eternal, as God is eternal. "He was in the beginning with God" and participated in the work of creation. (John 1:1-3) "He shall reign forever and ever." (Revelation 11:15)

Scriptures call him God. "Thomas answered him, 'My Lord and my God.'" (John 20:28) "This [Jesus] is the true God and eternal life." (1 John 5:20) Read Hebrews 1.

The Christian Church confesses him to be God. Note the particular stress which the Nicene Creed (page 148) places on this article of Christian faith.

TRUE MAN

In God's appointed time, some twenty centuries ago, Christ became a man, born of Virgin Mary. "The Word became flesh and dwelt among us." (John 1:14) God, in the person of Christ, paid our world a visit, became our brother, entered into our struggle for existence, shared our joys and sorrows and even our temptations. Christmas is the celebration of God's incarnation (taking on human flesh), the most amazing event in world history. "Great indeed, we confess, is the mystery of our religion: He was manifested in the flesh, vindicated in the Spirit, seen by angels, preached among the nations, believed on in the world, taken up in glory." (I Timothy 3:16)

Jesus most frequently called himself the Son of Man. Besides being a title for the promised Messiah, this name serves to remind us of his humanity. Our Messiah needed to be a man to live as we do under God's law and judgment. "God sent forth his Son, born of woman, born under the law, to redeem those who were under the law." (Galatians 4:4-5) He had to be a man to suffer and die sacrificially for us. He needed to be a brother who would know from experience our temptations, weaknesses and limitations as mortal people. As the Son of Man he sympathizes with us in our weaknesses. "We have not a high priest who is unable to sympathize with our weaknesses, but one who in every respect has been tempted as we are, yet without sin." (Hebrews 4:15) He prays, indeed intercedes, for us. (Romans 8:34) As the Son of Man who walked on earth he left footprints which mark the path for his followers.

The Mission of Christ

In Adam and Eve we have a picture of what God intended people to be. Sin ruined the picture. Christ, the second Adam, is more than another picture of God's ideal person. He came to make the picture a reality. Christ is not just the perfect person after whom we must try to pattern our lives. His mission was to restore to people the life which they lost by falling into sin. Christ, as we have noted, often spoke of his mission in terms of bringing people life. The Son of God entered into people's life so that they might enter into his life as children of God. "To all who received him, who believed in his name, he gave power to become children of God." (John 1:12) As God-man, Christ was preeminently equipped to restore the broken relationship between God and people. He was an intermediary who acted for both God and people.

A biblical study of the mission of Christ requires regarding him as the Messiah in whom Old Testament prophecy was fulfilled. The various phases of his messianic work are traditionally and best treated in terms of his threefold office, as our prophet, our priest and our king.

CHRIST, OUR PROPHET

Biblical prophets were God's messengers who proclaimed to people the judgments, promises and instruction they received from him. Their prophecies (what they "spoke forth") related not only to the future but also to the past and, in largest measure, to the present.

The Lord Jesus was a prophet without a peer. As one sent from God, he made God known to people. "No one has ever seen God; the only Son, who is in the bosom of the Father, he has made him known [to us]." (John 1:18) Jesus not only proclaimed the word of God but was the Word. (John 1:1-5) He made God known to us not only by what he said but also by the kind of person he was, what he did, and what he suffered. The special knowledge he gave us was about God's amazing kindness. God gave the law through Moses, but "grace and truth came through Jesus Christ." (John 1:17)

The Son of God's death on the cross, which was God's sacrifice for the sins of all people, reveals most clearly God's boundless love for sinful people. "God so loved the world that he gave his only Son." (John 3:16) "God shows his love for us in that while we were yet sinners Christ died for us." (Romans 5:8)

By raising his Son from the dead God revealed his power to raise people from the death of sin to a life of righteousness. "If the Spirit of him who raised Jesus from the dead dwells in you, he who raised Christ Jesus from the dead will give life to your mortal bodies also through his Spirit which dwells in you." (Romans 8:11)

CHRIST, OUR PRIEST

The duties of the priest in the Old Testament related primarily to the offering of sacrifices. Sacrifices were offered as gifts to God and as acts of atonement for sin. The only sins, however, for which they could atone were ritual sins committed in ignorance, failure to follow the "fine print" of the law while performing acts of worship, which could scarcely be called sin. For real sins there was no forgiveness by sacrifice. The apostle says, "It is impossible that the blood of bulls and goats should take away sins." (Hebrews 10:4) The office of the Old Testament high priest is not a true picture but only a shadow, or a faint outline, of what our high priest, the Lord Jesus, accomplished.

We need a high priest who is "holy, blameless, unstained, separated from sinners, exalted above the heavens." (Hebrews 7:26) Part of our Lord's mission was to keep the law of God that we are always breaking. It is by Christ's complete obedience to the will of God that we are made righteous. "For as by one man's disobedience many were made sinners, so by one man's obedience many will be made righteous." (Romans 5:19)

We need a high priest who could make an effectual sacrifice for sin. This Jesus did by offering up, not the blood of animals, but his own precious blood in atonement for the sins of all people. The high priest himself became the lamb "that takes away the sin of the world." (John 1:29) The effectual sacrifice for sin that human beings could never make, God made for them by the sacrifice of his Son on Calvary. God designed his death to be the means by which people's sins are forgiven. "The blood of Jesus Christ his Son cleanses us from all sin." (1 John 1:7) It was the once-for-all-people-and-times sacrifice for sin. "Christ had offered for all time a single sacrifice for sins." (Hebrews 10:12)

CHRIST, OUR KING

Although Jesus was a descendent of the illustrious King David, as messianic prophecy required, he was a far different kind of king. David, like other kings, established his kingdom by waging wars. Jesus was the Prince of Peace who established his kingdom not by killing but by dying for people. David was popular because of the political and economic advantages Israel enjoyed under his rule. Jesus was unpopular because he refused to be a military leader or bread-king.

What kind of king is he? Paul says, "The kingdom of God does not mean food and drink but righteousness and peace and joy in the Holy Spirit." (Romans 14:17) When Pontius Pilate questioned Jesus about his kingship, he said, "My kingship is not of this world; if my kingship were of this world, my servants would fight, that I might not be handed over to the Jews; but my kingship is not from the world." When Pilate went on to ask, "So you are a king?" Jesus replied, "You say that I am a king. For this I was born.... Every one who is of the truth hears my voice." (John 18:36-37) The kingship of Christ embraces people of all generations who have accepted his word and worshipped him as Savior and Lord. These are the subjects over whom he rules with his forgiving love and with whom he shares his rule. The people he ransomed for God by his blood he made "a kingdom and priests to God, and they shall reign on earth." (Revelation 5:10)

The Bible further affirms that God placed Christ "far above all rule and authority and power and dominion, and above every name that is named, not only in this age but also in that which is to come; and he has put all things under his feet." (Ephesians 1:21-22) Jesus said, "All authority in heaven and on earth has been given to me." (Matthew 28:18)

When Christ appears again in glory every knee will bow at his name, and every tongue will confess that he is Lord. (Philippians 2:8-11)

Talking It Over

Use each of the following statements as a basis for discussion.

1. —how God made the Israelites his people

2. —what the New Testament affirms of Jesus as the promised Messiah

3. —the similarities and differences between Adam and Jesus

4. —biblical reasons for believing Jesus to be God

5. —the importance of knowing Christ as a true man

6. —why our Savior and Life-giver needed to be the God-man

7. —the sense in which Christ is our prophet

8. —the sense in which he is our priest

9. —the sense in which he is our king

True and False Statements

Circle the letter **T** for true statements and the letter **F** for false statements.

T   F   1. The two testaments of the Bible refer to two covenants which God made with his people.

T   F   2. God's covenants, like human covenants, are on a tit-for-tat basis: "You serve me and I'll serve you."

T   F   3. The Old Testament people of God believed in him as their Savior because he delivered them out of Egypt and made a covenant with them on Mt. Sinai. Christians believe the same thing about God for a different reason.

T   F   4. What God promised his people in the Old Testament was never fulfilled because of their sinfulness.

T   F   5. Jesus was the son of God in exactly the same way that Adam was.

T   F   6. When our Lord became man he ceased to be God.

T   F   7. It is possible for people to believe in Christ as their Savior without believing him to be God.

T   F   8. Jesus was like every other human being except that he was sinless.

T   F   9. It is comforting to know that Christ is still a man and our brother.

T   F   10. A Christian is a person who believes that Jesus was the perfect human being whom they must imitate.

T   F   11. Prophet, in the Bible, means a person who predicts the future.

T   F   12. Christ's office as a prophet is to change people's thoughts about God and themselves.

T   F   13. The purpose of Old Testament sacrifices was to atone for sin.

T   F   14. Christians are still required to make sacrifices to atone for sin.

T   F   15. Christ was a king like David.

T   F   16. Christ rules not only over believers but over everyone.

Bible Reading

The Gospel of Luke
Chapters 1-12

A Prayer for Discipleship

Lord Jesus,
      you are the way,
           and the truth,
                and the life.
Guide our feet,
      keeping us on the path marked by your footsteps.
Inform our minds,
      bending them to obedient trust in your word.
Remove from our hearts
      the gloom of sin and death by sharing with us the
      victory you won over them.
In your name we ask it.

THE MILESTONES
OF OUR LORD'S LIFE

PREVIEW

We shall now pause briefly at the milestones in our Lord's life mentioned in the second article of the Apostles' Creed, with particular emphasis on his resurrection from death as the foundation of Christian faith. We shall then review the terms used in the New Testament to describe the new life in Christ.

The Statements of the Apostles' Creed

"CONCEIVED BY THE HOLY SPIRIT, BORN OF THE VIRGIN MARY"

Although the virgin birth of Jesus, related in the Christmas stories of Matthew and Luke, is never mentioned again in the New Testament, it does have significance for the church. It affirms that this was in every way a supernatural birth in which God was at work. It further testifies to Jesus as being the true Son of God. The greater Adam, like the first Adam, had no other father but God. The angel, who announced to Mary that she would conceive and bear a son, said, "The child to be born will be called holy, the Son of God." (Luke 1:35) It was natural for Jesus to call God his father as, indeed, was his custom.

"SUFFERED UNDER PONTIUS PILATE"

Nearly one-third of the story of Christ's life in the four Gospels is devoted to his suffering. Of all the Old Testament pictures or types of the Messiah, that of Isaiah's suffering servant of God, which people chose to ignore, matched him most perfectly. He suffered innocently and vicariously, "for our transgressions." His suffering was fruitful, resulting in many being accounted righteous. Read Isaiah 53.

"For our sake God made him to be sin who knew no sin, so that in him we might become the righteousness of God." (2 Corinthians 5:21) God treated him, who was righteous, as a sinner, so that he might treat us, who are sinners, as righteous people.

"CRUCIFIED, DEAD, BURIED"

Jesus paid for us the wages of sin which is death. (Romans 6:23) He suffered for us the pangs of spiritual death which is separation from God. He cried out on the cross, "My God, my God, why hast thou forsaken me?" (Matthew 27:46), so that we might forever have God with us. He then died physically. (Matthew 27:50) His death on the cross was perpetrated by people but was also planned by God to be an offering for the sins of all people. "This Jesus, delivered up according to the definite plan and foreknowledge of God, you crucified and killed by the hands of lawless men." (Acts 2:23) We are all to blame for it and we all stand to benefit by it.

"HE DESCENDED INTO HELL"

Traditionally the church has taken these words to mean that Christ proclaimed himself to be the victor over the occupants of hell. The single biblical passage (1 Peter 3:18-20) on which this thought is based admits of various interpretations. An optional wording is, "He went to the dead."

"ON THE THIRD DAY HE AROSE AGAIN"

The most wonderful thing about our Lord's life is that it does not end with the words, "dead and buried." Our creed goes on to say, "The third day he arose again from the dead." We worship the living Christ who died and is alive for evermore. (Revelation 1:18) The climax of each of the four Gospels is the Easter story. (Matthew 28; Mark 16; Luke 24; John 20) The resurrected Christ appeared to his disciples on several occasions. (1 Corinthians 15:3-8)

The Foundations of Our Christian Faith

The resurrection of Christ, celebrated by the church not only in the Easter season but every Sunday or Lord's Day, is the foundation of our Christian faith. St. Paul states this truth negatively in the words, "If Christ has not been raised, your faith is futile and you are still in your sins. Then those who have fallen asleep in Christ have perished." (1 Corinthians 15:17-18)

The resurrection removes all doubts about (1) his person, (2) his words and promises, and (3) his work as our Redeemer and Life-giver.

1. "He was designated Son of God in power according to the Spirit of holiness by his resurrection from the dead." (Romans 1:4)

2. "As the first-born of the dead Jesus Christ is a faithful witness." (Revelation 1:5) His words are "the words of the first and the last, who died and came to life." (Revelation 2:8)

3. Righteousness "will be reckoned to us who believe in him that raised from the dead Jesus our Lord, who was put to death for our trespasses and raised for our

justification." (Romans 4:24-25) This means that our finding favor with God depended on Christ, our representative. Thus God's raising him from the dead means our justification (our being on right terms with God). Our faith in God's willingness and power to raise us from death to life, physically and spiritually, rests on the fact that he raised Jesus from the dead.

In the explanation of the second article of the Apostles' Creed (page 133), Luther speaks of the blessings of the believer's new life in Christ and concludes with the words, "even as he is risen from the dead, lives and rules to all eternity." Because he lives we live also. (John 14:19)

TWO RESURRECTIONS

The Easter message is the basis for the believer's hope of two resurrections: a spiritual resurrection from the death of sin to a life of righteousness and a bodily resurrection when Christ returns to earth at the end of time.

"Jesus said to her, 'I am the resurrection and the life; he who believes in me, though he die, yet shall he live and whoever lives and believes in me shall never die.' " (John 11:25-26)

"Christ Jesus...abolished death and brought life and immortality to light through the Gospel." (2 Timothy 1:10)

"The hour is coming when all who are in the tombs will hear his voice and come forth, those who have done good to the resurrection of life, and those who have done evil, to the resurrection of judgment." (John 5:28-29) Read St. Paul's resurrection chapter, 1 Corinthians 15.

"HE ASCENDED INTO HEAVEN"

Heaven is primarily not a place but a condition. It is the complete enjoyment of God's presence which life in this sinful world can never afford.

Christ's ascension into heaven does not mean that he departed from this world. One of his last words to his disciples was, "Lo, I am with you always, to the close of the ages." (Matthew 28:20) Neither does his ascension mean that his work on earth came to an end. On the contrary, it is the assurance of the continuance of his redemptive work through the church over which he now rules. His last command to his disciples was "Go therefore and make disciples of all nations, baptizing them in the name of the Father and of the Son and of the Holy Spirit, teaching them to observe all that I have commanded you." (Matthew 28:19-20) The ascension of Christ is the glorious climax of the life which he shares with his followers. "Where I am," he said, "there shall my servant be also." (John 12:26) He entered into the glory of his Father as our forerunner. He said, "In my Father's house are many rooms; if it were not so, would I have told you that I go to prepare a place for you?" (John 14:2)

"HE SITS AT THE RIGHT HAND OF GOD"

The right hand of God, an expression used frequently in the Old Testament, pictures a position of ultimate kingly honor and power. He who rules above all the turmoil and confusion of our world is our brother who died for us and intercedes for us. "Who is to condemn? It is Christ Jesus, who died, yes, who was raised from the dead, who is at the right hand of God, who indeed intercedes for us?" (Romans 8:34) Serving him the church is sure of success. "The powers of death shall not prevail against it." (Matthew 16:18) Fighting his battles the church already celebrates the victory.

"HE SHALL COME AGAIN TO JUDGE THE LIVING AND THE DEAD"

Christ's lordship, which is still a matter of faith, will be evident to all people when he comes again visibly and in glory to judge the world. A description of the Final Judgment which embraces all of God's judgments is given in Matthew 24 and 25.

Following are some pertinent biblical truths about Judgment Day.

1. No one knows when it will be. (Matthew 24:27)

2. Signs of its nearness have all been fulfilled. (Matthew 24:3-14)

3. Believers are to be in constant readiness for it. (Matthew 24:44; 25:1-13)

4. To believers Christ's coming in glory means the full realization of their redemption. "Now when these things begin to take place, look up and raise your heads, because your redemption is drawing near." (Luke 21:28) It will be their wedding day, the coming of the bridegroom to carry his bride, the church, across the threshold of the mansion he has prepared for them.

5. People will be judged by what they did or did not do for Christ. (Matthew 25:31-46) A living faith will produce deeds of mercy and love. "Faith, by itself, if it has no works, is dead." (James 2:17)

6. Judgment Day will not change anything in our essential relationship to God. Those who live with Christ now will live with him in the hereafter. Those who live apart from Christ on earth will be sentenced to live apart from him in eternity. (Matthew 25:41)

Biblical Words Describing the New Life

The Bible uses many different words to describe our new life in Christ.

1. We enjoy forgiveness of sins.

"Let it be known to you therefore, brethren, that through this man forgiveness of sins is proclaimed to you." (Acts 13:38)

2. We have salvation. We have been delivered from sin, death and the devil. Although we are assailed by them we are no longer under their power.

"For to you is born this day in the city of David a Savior, who is Christ the Lord." (Luke 2:11)

"There is salvation in no one else, for there is no other name under heaven given among men by which we must be saved." (Acts 4:12)

"O death, where is thy victory? O death, where is thy sting? The sting of death is sin, and the power of sin is the law. But thanks be to God, who gives us the victory through our Lord Jesus Christ." (1 Corinthians 15:55-57)

The Father "has delivered us from the dominion of darkness and transferred us to the kingdom of his beloved Son." (Colossians 1:13)

3. We are redeemed. Christ ransomed us from our kidnappers. The reference in the Bible is to the payment of a price to secure a benefit, especially to free or acquire a slave.

"You know that you were ransomed from the futile ways inherited from your fathers, not with perishable things such as silver or gold, but with the precious blood of Christ, like that of a lamb without blemish or spot." (1 Peter 1:18-19)

"Thou wast slain and by thy blood didst ransom men for God." (Revelation 5:9)

4. God has justified us. He has declared us to be innocent and righteous for Christ's sake despite our guilt.

"Who shall bring any charge against God's elect? It is God who justifies; who is to condemn?" (Romans 8:33-34)

"A man is not justified by works of the law but through faith in Jesus Christ." (Galatians 2:16)

5. We possess God's righteousness. The believer in Christ is clothed with his righteousness. Luther said that St. Paul's pet expression, "the righteousness of God," once frightened him because he thought it meant the righteousness God required of him. When he came to realize that it meant the righteousness God freely offered in Christ, he was "new-born and in paradise." Righteousness in the Bible means everything God our Savior did to make us righteous. It implies that

Christ saved us not only from something but also for something, namely, to be righteous.

"As by one man's disobedience many were made sinners, so by one man's obedience many will be made righteous." (Romans 5:19)

"For his sake I have suffered the loss of all things, and count them as refuse, in order that I may gain Christ, and be found in him, not having a righteousness of my own, based on law, but that which is through faith in Christ, the righteousness of God that depends on faith." (Philippians 3:8-9)

6. We are reconciled to God. Once God's enemies because of our sins we are now his friends.

"We also rejoice in God through our Lord Jesus Christ, through whom we have now received our reconciliation." (Romans 5:11)

"God was in Christ reconciling the world to himself, not counting their trespasses against them, and entrusting to us the message of reconciliation." (2 Corinthians 5:19)

7. We enjoy life. We are God's beloved children who cry, "Abba! Father!...and if children, then heirs, heirs of God and fellow heirs with Christ." (Romans 8:15-17)

PUBLISHING THE GOOD NEWS

That Christ by his life, death and resurrection merited these blessings for all people is the Gospel or good news, which the church has been commissioned by its Lord to broadcast to the ends of the earth and that people must believe to be saved. "I am not ashamed of the Gospel: it is the power of God for salvation to every one who has faith." (Romans 1:16)

"We are ambassadors for Christ, God making his appeal through us. We beseech you on behalf of Christ, be reconciled to God." (2 Corinthians 5:20)

How can we help but share with non-Christians the thrilling good news of all that Christ did for us and them?

Talking It Over

Use each of the following statements and questions as a basis for discussion.

1. —the significance of the virgin birth of Jesus in St. Luke's Christmas story

2. —the unappealing but true picture of Christ in Isaiah 53

3. In what two ways did Christ die?

4. —the importance of the Easter message

5. —the two resurrections of believers that result from Christ's resurrection

6. What does Christ's ascension into heaven not mean? What does it mean?

7. What does his sitting at the right hand of God mean?

8. What are some important biblical truths about Judgment Day?

9. —prominent biblical words which describe the Christian's blessings

10. —the importance of spreading the Gospel, and ways of doing it

True and False Statements

Circle the letter **T** for true statements and the letter **F** for false statements.

T F 1. The virgin birth of Jesus is often spoken of in the New Testament.

T F 2. The death of Jesus was planned by both God and sinful people.

T F 3. The violent death of Jesus brings to light God's anger with sinful people.

T F 4. The words of the Creed, "He descended into hell," were intended to mean that Jesus suffered all the tortures of hell.

T F 5. All people are to blame for the death of Christ and all were benefited by it.

T F 6. Since God offered his Son as a sacrifice for people's sins, no one is required to offer any more sacrifices for sin.

T F 7. Even if Christ had not risen from the dead we would have forgiveness of sins and life with God.

T F 8. The comfort of the Easter story is that it makes certain there will be a physical resurrection for all people.

T F 9. At least 500 people saw Jesus after his resurrection.

T F 10. Christ cannot be present with us since he ascended into heaven.

T F 11. All that we know about the location of heaven is that it is up.

T F 12. Christ's "sitting at the right hand of God" means that having finished his work, he now enjoys rest.

T F 13. Christ will return to earth in a visible form.

T F 14. All the signs of the nearness of Judgment Day given in the Bible are apparent today.

T F 15. People will be judged by their deeds, regardless of what they believed.

T F 16. Christians should live as though each day may be their last day on earth.

T F 17. Everyone has reason to be afraid of Judgment Day.

T F 18. Preaching the Gospel is only the pastor's business.

For Further Study

Match these biblical words with their definitions.

_____ Life

_____ Redemption

_____ Reconciliation

_____ Justification

_____ Righteousness of God

_____ Salvation

1. Enemies of God made friends.

2. Fellowship with God and service under God.

3. God declaring the guilty sinner to be righteous.

4. What God did through Christ to make people righteous.

5. Christ's payment of the price required to free us from the slavery of sin and place us in God's kingdom.

6. Deliverance from sin, death and the devil.

Bible Reading

The Gospel of Luke
Chapters 13-24.

An Easter Prayer

O Lord Jesus Christ,
>who rose victorious from the dead
>conquering for us death and the grave
>and opening to us the gates of
>everlasting life:

>receive, we pray,
>our adoration and praise for this
>victory which you have obtained for us,
>and grant that we may always follow
>you the way,
>hold fast to you the truth, and live
>now and eternally in you the life,
>who with the Father and the Holy Spirit,
>lives and reigns, one God
>forever.

7

SHARING CHRIST'S LIFE

BY FAITH

PREVIEW

The question for which we now need an answer is, "How do we come to share in Christ's victorious life?"

The purpose of Christ's coming into the world was to bring people life. Christ fulfilled his mission. "It is accomplished," he said just before he died on the cross. By his life, death and resurrection he made life possible for all people.

God earnestly wants all people to enjoy this life. "As I live, says the Lord God, I have no pleasure in the death of the wicked, but that the wicked turn from his way and live." (Ezekiel 33:11)

What God desires he strives to bring about. He invites people to share in all the blessings of Christ's redemptive work. He made and still makes all the necessary provisions for them to accept his invitation.

It is this ongoing work of God, which the New Testament commonly ascribes to the Holy Spirit, that we shall now discuss.

The Importance of Faith

FAITH, THE VITAL LINK

The problem we are concerned about is establishing a connection between Christ and us. Christ's death and resurrection are ancient history. Centuries and continents separate us from them. How can they solve our problems? "God sent his only Son into the world, so that we might live through him." (1 John 4:9) How do we get to live through him?

Between the oxygen tank and the person who has ceased breathing there must be an instrument to convey the oxygen to his or her lungs. What is the link that connects the person who is dead in sin with Christ, the Life-giver?

The Bible says it is faith. Faith puts us in connection with Christ. It is the hand that opens up to accept his gift of salvation. By believing in Christ we experience that he is our Redeemer and Life-giver.

"God so loved the world that he gave his only Son, that whoever believes in him should not perish but have eternal life." (John 3:16)

"These [things] are written that you may believe that Jesus is the Christ, the Son of God, and that believing you may have life in his name." (John 20:31)

FAITH, THE PROPER RESPONSE

There is nothing new about the New Testament emphasis on faith. We discussed the importance of faith in God, the creator of life, in Lesson 3. The children of God in every age were believers in God. Read Hebrews 11. Just as there can be no proper marital relationship without trust, so neither can there be a right relationship with God without faith. The proper way for a person to respond to all of God's works and words is by believing. Believing in Christ is saying "yes and amen" to God's most wonderful and gracious work of redemption.

Christ compared the kingdom of God to a banquet (Luke 14:16-24) and a marriage feast. (Matthew 22:1-14) The host is God who through his servants invites people to enjoy his gracious hospitality. The food is forgiveness, salvation and life purchased by Christ. Believers are guests who have accepted the invitation.

St. Paul insists on faith as being the only proper response to the good news of what Christ did for us because the Gospel is a promise that God makes to us. (Romans 4:13-16) We can do only one of two things with a promise: believe it or not believe it.

"The Gospel," someone has said, "does not bring us a work to do but a word to believe about a work that has been done."

FAITH, NOT WORKS

The Biblical teaching that it is only by faith in Christ that a person enters into a right relationship with God stands in diametric opposition to the common false hope of being able to befriend God by keeping his laws and leading a good life. To begin with, people who are dead in sin are utterly incapable of keeping God's law. Their problem is that they are law-breakers. The law, therefore, is their problem and not the solution. The law does not bring people life. It condemns and kills them. St. Paul says, "The very commandment which promised life proved to be death to me. For sin, finding opportunity in the commandment, deceived me and by it killed me." (Romans 7:10-11) Believing in Christ requires surrendering the old "do it yourself" religion which our proud flesh delights in. This is not an indictment of the evident morality of many non-Christian people. It is simply saying with St. Paul that "all have sinned and fallen short of the glory of God" and need to be "justified by his grace as a free gift." (Romans 3:23-24)

What It Means to Believe

FAITH PRESUPPOSES KNOWLEDGE

We cannot believe in anyone we do not know about. "How are they to believe in him of whom they have not heard?" (Romans 10:14) God provided that people should know about Christ through the preaching of the Gospel. For this purpose he commanded the Gospel to be preached, instituted Baptism, ordained the ministry and established the church.

FAITH IMPLIES FORSAKING SIN

The words *repent* and *believe* are frequently found together in the New Testament. Faith implies a right attitude toward God, recognizing him as God, turning to him for salvation. But before people can turn to God they must repent, which means they must turn away from sin. There is a new life with God to be entered; there is an old self-centered life to be given up.

"If anyone is in Christ, he is a new creation; the old has passed away, behold, the new has come." (2 Corinthians 5:17)

FAITH PERCEIVES GOD'S LOVE

A person might know something of God's power and holiness without having Christian faith. Faith in Christ, who died for us, opens our eyes to the forgiving love of God to which our guilt had formerly blinded us. In nature we see God above us. In law we see him against us. In Christ we see him with us.

"In this the love of God was made manifest among us, that God sent his only Son into the world, so that we might live through him. In this is love, not that we loved God but that he loved us and sent his Son to be the expiation for our sins." (1 John 4:9-10)

FAITH PRODUCES A NEW LIFE

Faith is not merely a matter of the mind and lips, but also of the heart and life. It is productive of good works ("Faith apart from works is barren."—James 2:20); purity ("Every one who thus hopes in him [God] purifies himself as he is pure."—1 John 3:3); and love for people ("Beloved, let us love one another; for love is of God, and he who loves is born of God and knows God."—1 John 4:7).

FAITH IS A GIFT OF GOD

In his explanation of the third article of the Apostles' Creed (page 142), Luther teaches us to say, "I believe that I cannot by my own understanding or effort believe in Jesus Christ, my Lord, or come to him."

Christian faith is not a human achievement or accomplishment. Being dead in sin rules out the possibility of people becoming believers by their own effort. Again it is a case of God coming to the rescue. Faith in Christ is his work and gift. The same God who created the light of the universe must create in our hearts the light of the knowledge of Christ. "It is the God who said, 'Let light shine out of darkness,' who has shone in our hearts to give the light of the knowledge of the glory of God in the face of Christ." (2 Corinthians 4:6)

"By grace you have been saved through faith; and this is not your own doing, it is the gift of God." (Ephesians 2:8)

The Holy Spirit, the Giver of Life

This ongoing work of God of bringing people to faith in Christ, which accounts for the existence and growth of the Christian church, is the activity of the third person of the Godhead, the Holy Spirit.

"No one can say Jesus is Lord except by the Holy Spirit." (1 Corinthians 12:3)

The Nicene Creed (page 148) calls the Holy Spirit "the Lord and Giver of Life." The Spirit's gift of faith in Christ is the gift of life with God.

The Holy Spirit does more than bring people to faith in Jesus Christ. He keeps them in the faith and enables them to live as children of God.

Luther explains the work of the Holy Spirit in the words, "The Holy Spirit has called me through the Gospel, enlightened me with his gifts, and sanctified and kept me in true faith. In the same way he calls, gathers, enlightens, and sanctifies the whole Christian church on earth, and keeps it united with Jesus Christ in the one true faith." Sanctification is God's process of making us holy.

THE CHRISTIAN'S DRIVING POWER

The Holy Spirit is to the believer what an engine is to an automobile. Read Romans 8:9-28 and note what is said about the Holy Spirit. He is the Spirit of God who dwells in believers and gives them the spirit of Christ, making them alive. He rules over their lives, enabling them to overcome their sinful desires. He assures them that they are the children of God and, together with Christ, heirs of God. He fills their hearts with a yearning but sure hope of complete deliverance from bodily distresses. He helps them to pray aright and even intercedes for them.

Jesus promised his disciples that upon his departure the Holy Spirit would take his place in their lives, enabling them to do the works he did. "I will pray the Father, and

he will give you another Counselor, to be with you for ever, even the Spirit of truth."
(John 14:16) "He who believes in me will also do the works that I do; and greater
works than these will he do." (John 14:12) The Acts of the Apostles record a
fulfillment of this prophecy. From beginning to end the apostles and their followers
are Spirit-driven. Typical passages are Acts 1:8; 2:4; 10:19-20; 13:2; 16:6.

THE HOLY SPIRIT WORKS THROUGH THE GOSPEL

The Holy Spirit performs his life-giving work on people through the Gospel. By
confronting them with the message of God's love in Christ, who died for them and
rose again, the Holy Spirit plants the seed of faith in their hearts. The same Gospel
also nourishes Christian faith and causes it to grow. Without the Gospel a person can
neither become nor remain a believer in Christ.

"So faith comes from what is heard, and what is heard comes by the preaching of
Christ." (Romans 10:17)

"I am not ashamed of the Gospel: it is the power of God for salvation to every one
who has faith." (Romans 1:16)

THE FESTIVAL OF PENTECOST

The church celebrates the work of the Holy Spirit at Pentecost, one of its three major
festivals. Pentecost celebrates what is often called the birthday of the Christian
church. The story is told in Acts 2.

The Pure Grace of God

St. Paul said, "By the grace of God I am what I am." (1 Corinthians 15:10) This gives
all the credit for being a Christian to God. Christ did everything necessary to put us
into a right relationship with God. The Holy Spirit does all that is necessary to
establish the blessed faith relationship with Christ.

Grace excludes boasting or laying even the slightest claim on God's favor on the
basis of what we deserve or earn. The Christian is God's creation, his workmanship,
the living building he planned and constructed.

"By grace you have been saved through faith; and this is not your own doing, it is the
gift of God—not because of works, lest any man should boast. For we are his
workmanship, created in Christ Jesus for good works, which God prepared be-
forehand, that we should walk in them." (Ephesians 2:8-10)

Note the contrast here between the Christian religion and the religion of human
reason. Christians believe in salvation by God's grace, through faith, all of it being a

gift of God and resulting in giving all glory to God. Non-Christians think salvation is a matter of their own doing, of good deeds and sacrifices, resulting in boastfulness.

THE MIRACLE OF ST. PAUL'S CONVERSION

St. Paul emphasized God's grace in the making of a Christian because his own conversion from a persecutor of the church to a believer and zealous missionary was so obviously a miracle of God's grace. Read Acts 9:1-20.

OUR CONVERSION

Although most Christians have a less dramatic story to tell about their regeneration, all Christians must finally say with St. Paul, "By the grace of God I am what I am." Your story may be: born of Christian parents, brought to Christ in baptism as an infant, taught the word of God as a child. All glory to God! Or it may be: married a Christian spouse or was led by God to a Christian friend who shared his or her faith with me. All glory to God!

GRACE CAN BE SPURNED

To say that a person is saved by God's grace further implies that the Holy Spirit does not force anyone to believe in Christ against his or her will. As Luther said, "God does not drag people into heaven by the hair." People can say no to God's offer of life. They can turn down God's invitation. Jesus complained, "O Jerusalem, Jerusalem, killing the prophets and stoning those who are sent to you! How often would I have gathered your children together as a hen gathers her brood under her wings, and you would not!" (Matthew 23:37) The Holy Spirit can be resisted. (Acts 7:51) People cannot make a flower grow. The soil, the seed, the food and water are gifts of God. But people have many ways of causing flowers not to grow. The seed of God's word, which is able to save our souls (James 1:21), suffers various fates. Read Luke 8:4-15.

LIFE RESTORED MAY DIE AGAIN

The grace of God can be accepted in vain. (2 Corinthians 6:1) The Holy Spirit dwelling in a believer can be driven out (Psalm 51:11) or quenched. (1 Thessalonians 5:19) The devil driven out may return. (Luke 11:24-26) Followers of Christ can forsake him. (Luke 8:13; John 6:66)

COOPERATING WITH THE HOLY SPIRIT

Believers must continually cooperate with the Holy Spirit. The faith he implants must, like a flower, be diligently watered and nourished. The word of God is the food that sustains Christian life. "Man shall not live by bread alone, but by every word that proceeds from the mouth of God." (Matthew 4:4) Christians must cooperate with the Holy Spirit by faithfully hearing and reading the word of God, communing with God in private and public workshop, praying, partaking of the Lord's Supper, seeking the companionship of other Christians for mutual strength and inquiring after the will of God at every crossroad in life. When these practices are neglected, faith dies and the Spirit is quenched.

Talking It Over

Use each of the following statements as a basis for discussion.

1. —the importance of believing in Christ

2. —what old thoughts and ways a person must give up to become a believer

3. —the biblical definition of saving faith

4. —the work of the Holy Spirit

5. —what the Bible means by saying we are saved by God's grace

6. —why, despite God's grace, many are not Christians

7. —how a person must cooperate with the Holy Spirit

True and False Statements

Circle the letter **T** for true statements and the letter **F** for false statements.

T   F   1. God accomplished his life-giving work in Christ twenty centuries ago and it is now up to us to make the most of it.

T   F   2. It is by sincerely trying to love God and people that a person enters into a right relationship with God.

T   F   3. Human reason always leads people to believe that getting on right terms with God is a matter of their own doing.

T   F   4. The Holy Spirit does nothing more than invite people to believe in Christ.

T   F   5. A Christian is a creation of God.

T   F   6. Pentecost is less important than Easter because the work of the Holy Spirit is secondary to that of Christ.

T   F   7. We should expect the Holy Spirit to do for us all that he did for the apostles of Christ.

T   F   8. A person can repent of sin without having faith in Christ.

T   F   9. Believing that God loves them is no great problem for people.

T   F   10. The biblical teaching that a person is saved by faith and not by his or her works means that good works are not necessary for salvation.

T   F   11. People do not have the power to accept God's invitation of life in Christ but they do have the power to turn it down.

T   F   12. "Saved by grace" means giving all of the credit to God for our Christian faith and life.

T   F   13. God gives us our Christian faith and only God may take it away from us.

T   F   14. Once a Christian, always a Christian.

T   F   15. The Holy Spirit always works with a tool, namely, the Gospel.

T   F   16. The word of God is to the believer what food is to the body.

T   F   17. There is nothing a person can do to acquire or preserve Christian faith.

For Further Study

Major changes, foreseen by the prophets of the Old Testament, took place in the church after Christ's resurrection.

- What was new about the mission of the church? Compare Peter's Pentecost sermon, especially Acts 2:17 and 38-39, with Isaiah 60:1-5.

- What was new about the message of the church? Compare Acts 2:38 with Romans 3:21-25.

Bible Reading

The Book of Acts
Chapters 1-7

A Prayer for the Gift of the Holy Spirit

God, the Father of our Lord Jesus Christ,
     as you sent upon the disciples the promised gift of the
     Holy Spirit, open our hearts to the power of the Spirit.
Kindle in us the fire of your love and strengthen our lives
     for service in your kingdom;
     through your Son,
Jesus Christ, our Lord.

8

BAPTISM —

THE WATER OF LIFE

PREVIEW

The Holy Spirit is the Giver of life. For many people his life-giving work began with their Baptism when, in the words of our Lord, they were "born of the water and the Spirit." (John 3:5) In this chapter we shall talk about the sacrament of Holy Baptism.

The Meaning of the Word Sacrament

Something needs to be said about the word *sacrament*. It never occurs in the Bible. Its literal meaning is simply a sacred act. Any solemn act performed by the church (marriage, for example) might be called a sacrament. This definition may be limited to mean a physical act which has spiritual significance, something like a kiss which means, "I love you." This may further be limited to mean a sacred act commanded by Christ which offers his gifts of forgiveness, life and salvation. Sacraments, in this last sense, are the saving Gospel in action. According to this definition there are, as we shall see, only two sacraments, Baptism and the Lord's Supper. Different definitions account for different answers to the question, "How many sacraments are there?"

The Origin of Baptism

The first mention of baptism in the New Testament is with reference to John whose mission was to prepare the way for Christ. He is called "the baptizer." Crowds were baptized by him in the river Jordan, confessing their sins.

JOHN'S BAPTISM AND CHRISTIAN BAPTISM

Read Mark 1:1-5. John's baptism appears similar to the standard practice of baptizing Gentiles who adopted the Jewish faith. It proclaimed that to become a true Israelite it was necessary to be wholly cleansed of sin and make radical changes in one's life (repent). Jesus himself was baptized of John, not to repent of sin, but to "fulfill all righteousness," to submit to all the laws and ordinances of God as every one's representative. Read Matthew 3:13-17. If there are similarities between John's baptism and Christian baptism, there are also important differences. See Acts 18:25 and 19:1-5.

Christian baptism owes its origin to the words of Christ, "All authority in heaven and on earth have been given to me. Go therefore and make disciples of all nations, baptizing them in the name of the Father and of the Son and of the Holy Spirit, teaching them to observe all that I have commanded you." (Matthew 28:18-20)

The Blessings of Baptism

Normally, Baptism marks the beginning of a person's new life in Christ. The day of Baptism is the Christian's birthday. Christ instituted Baptism as a means of making disciples. Through Baptism people, born of the flesh, receive a second birth of the Spirit which puts them into God's kingdom. Jesus said, "Truly, truly, I say to you, unless one is born of water and the Spirit, he cannot enter the kingdom of God." (John 3:5) In Baptism a person puts on Christ as a garment. "As many of you as were baptized into Christ have put on Christ." (Galatians 3:27)
In Baptism God imparts the fruits of Christ's redemptive work. As water is used for cleansing, so Baptism washes away sins. "Rise and be baptized, and wash away your sins, calling on his name." (Acts 22:16) Baptism offers salvation. "Baptism...now saves you, not as a removal of dirt from the body but as an appeal to God for a clear conscience, through the resurrection of Jesus Christ." (1 Peter 3:21) This means being saved does not imply leading a sinless life. It means a clear conscience before God who does not hold our sins against us because being baptized we enjoy the benefits of Christ's resurrection.

Baptism joins us to the death and resurrection of Christ and thus liberates us from sin and death. "Do you not know that all of us who have been baptized into Christ Jesus were baptized into his death? We were buried therefore with him by baptism into death, so that as Christ was raised from the dead by the glory of the Father, we too might walk in newness of life. For if we have been united with him in a death like his, we shall certainly be united with him in a resurrection like his." (Romans 6:3-5)

The words spoken during Baptism, "I baptize you in the name of the Father and of the Son and of the Holy Spirit," mean that God is accepting the forgiven sinner into his fellowship. Baptism is the establishing of a covenant, similar to the covenant he made with the children of Israel, in which he declares, "From this time forth you are my child and I am your God and Father."

The Obligations of Baptism

Christ, who has all authority in heaven and on earth, commanded Baptism. To obey this command is a matter of highest duty. Where there is the will to be baptized nothing could be simpler than the performance. See 2 Kings 5:10-14.

Baptism, as a Gospel promise, requires faith. Yet faith is a gift of God. What God requires, he offers.

Baptism, as initiation into the Christian faith, presupposes growth in knowledge and life. Christ's complete command is to baptize and teach people to observe all that he commanded. (Matthew 28:18-20) When infants are baptized it is assumed that they will be taught the word of God and encouraged to live by it. In the case of adults, according to Lutheran custom, instruction in the Christian faith precedes the administration of Baptism.

Baptism requires a life of daily repentance. The promise of the heavenly Father's forgiving love must be claimed anew every day. Ever-present sin and guilt must be overcome through daily repentance. This means confessing our sins, but telling ourselves, "I am still and will always be a baptized and forgiven child of God," and praying for God's help to live a righteous life.

St. Paul speaks of the necessity of daily reliving our Baptism by saying that through Baptism we participate in Christ's death and resurrection. We reenact them in our daily life. Like him, we die to sin and rise to a new life of righteousness. What happened when we were baptized must happen over and over again in our lives. We must consider ourselves "dead to sin and alive to God in Christ Jesus." (Romans 6:11)

Baptism as new life determines the use we make of our gifts and talents, and the quality of our service in the routine of our lives.

Infant Baptism

The Church baptizes infants because, (1) Christ's command included them ("All nations"—Matthew 28:19); (2) born in a state of sin and spiritual death, they need to be born again; (3) Baptism is the means ordained by God for sharing with infants, who cannot be preached to, our life in Christ. Infant Baptism demonstrates most clearly the pure grace of God who adopts unknowing children into his family and promises them every blessing. It is God voting infants into membership with his church.

The requirement of faith by no means rules out the Baptism of infants. Remembering that faith is not an intellectual accomplishment but the gift of the Holy Spirit and that it describes a right relationship with God, it may rightly be said that a baptized infant can and does believe in God. Our Lord spoke of little ones believing in him. (Matthew 18:6)

Parents eager to share with their children their life in Christ will arrange to have them baptized as soon as possible after birth.

Although Baptism is the only means of grace God has given us for little children, we dare not conclude that children who die without Baptism will necessarily perish. We are bound by God's ordinances but he himself is not. No restriction should ever be put on his redeeming love.

SPRINKLING OR IMMERSION?

No special way to baptize is prescribed in the New Testament. The Greek word for *baptize* is the equivalent of *wash,* which may be done in several ways. Note how the word is used in Mark 7:3-4 and Hebrews 9:10, where washing and ablutions are translations of *baptismos.*

EMERGENCY BAPTISMS

Ordinarily Baptism is administered by the pastor in a church service. In emergencies any Christian may and should administer Baptism. All that is essential to Baptism is the use of water applied to the body and saying, "I baptize you in the name of the Father and of the Son and of the Holy Spirit." This may be preceded or followed by the Our Father, the Apostles' Creed, and other prayers.

SPONSORS

Having sponsors for baptized infants is a good custom which deserves being practiced even though it is not commanded in the Bible. In addition to serving as witnesses, sponsors assume responsibility for the Christian education of the God-child, especially if the parents should die or prove neglectful. They also remember the child in their prayers. These requirements limit the choice of sponsors to Christian people.

CONFIRMATION

Confirmation is an old church practice that has been retained by several major church bodies. Its purpose in the Lutheran church is to prepare baptized children, by instruction in biblical teaching, to participate fully in the life and work of the church. The completion of this course of study is celebrated in a public rite in which the candidates make a profession of the faith into which they have been baptized, thus confirming, or underscoring, the covenant God made with them at their baptism.

Read the instruction on Holy Baptism from Luther's Small Catechism (page 137). The blessings and obligations of Baptism are also set forth clearly in the rite of Holy Baptism found in Lutheran books of worship.

Talking It Over

Use each of the following statements as a basis for discussion.

1. —the meaning of the word *sacrament*

2. —the meaning of John's baptism

3. —the blessings of Baptism

4. —the obligations of Baptism

5. —the reasons for baptizing infants

6. —performing an emergency Baptism

7. —the reason for sponsors

8. —Confirmation

True and False Statements

Circle the letter **T** for true statements and the letter **F** for false statements.

T F 1. Marriage might be called a sacrament.

T F 2. In the sacraments ordained by Christ the Holy Spirit performs his saving work without making use of the Gospel.

T F 3. Baptism was commanded by Jesus.

T F 4. John was the first to practice Christian baptism.

T F 5. Through Baptism God actually imparts the blessings of Christ's redemption.

T F 6. Baptism makes a person a member of a church denomination.

T F 7. Nothing more is demanded of parents by Christ than that they have their children baptized.

T F 8. Every unbaptized person might rightly be called an unbeliever.

T F 9. Since infants are innocent they do not need to have their sins washed away.

T F 10. We know of no other way of sharing our blessings in Christ with infants besides Baptism.

T F 11. Through Baptism God adopts infants into his family even though they are not aware of what is happening.

T F 12. There is no sense in which it can be said that an infant believes in Christ.

T F 13. The blessings of Baptism are forfeited by failure to practice daily repentance.

T F 14. We are compelled to believe that infants who die without having been baptized are doomed to eternal death.

T F 15. It is not wrong to baptize by immersing the whole body but it is wrong to say no other Baptism is valid.

T F 16. Only the pastor should administer Holy Baptism.

T F 17. The Baptism of infants is not valid without sponsors.

T F 18. Only people who attend church should be chosen as sponsors.

T F 19. The main purpose of Confirmation is to offer young people Christian instruction.

Bible Reading

The Book of Romans
Chapters 1-8

A Prayer of Thanksgiving After Baptism

God,
the Father of our Lord Jesus Christ,
> we give you thanks for freeing your sons and daughters
> from the power of sin and for raising them up to a new
> life through this holy sacrament.

Pour your Holy Spirit upon these newly baptized persons:

the spirit of wisdom and understanding,
the spirit of counsel and might,
the spirit of knowledge and fear of the Lord,
the spirit of joy in your presence.

HE NEW LIFE IN CHRIST

PREVIEW

The subject we shall now discuss is right living or practical goodness. Earlier we said in effect, "Forget about your good works." This is the correct thing to say when the subject is, "How does a person get on right terms with God?" "A man is not justified by works of the law but through faith in Jesus Christ." (Galatians 2:16) Does this mean that the word of God is not concerned about our doing good works? By no means. It strives to bring us into a faith-relationship with God so that we can perform good works. "Without faith it is impossible to please him [God]." (Hebrews 11:6) A right relationship with God which the Bible calls life results in a life that is right.

What is Goodness?

GOODNESS IS GODLINESS

Oneness with God implies likeness to God in nature. "Like father, like child" applies to God's children. "Love is of God, and he who loves is born of God and knows God." (1 John 4:7) Goodness is catching God's goodness, as in a j-mirror, and reflecting it on our neighbors.

Jesus answered ethical questions by saying, "Look at God whose child you are." He said, "You, therefore, must be perfect, as your heavenly Father is perfect." (Matthew 5:48) "Be merciful, even as your Father is merciful." (Luke 6:36) The way God treats us is the way we must treat people. We must forgive as he forgives us, as Jesus teaches in the "Our Father." We must love as we are loved. "Beloved, if God so loved us, we also ought to love one another." (1 John 4:11)

GOODNESS IS CHRISTLIKENESS

Goodness is Christlikeness because he bore the very image of God (Hebrews 1:3) and made God's nature known to us. (John 1:18) "He who says he abides in him [Christ] ought to walk in the same way in which he walked." (1 John 2:6)

DEFINITION OF A GOOD DEED

A good deed is something learned from Christ that is done in loving response to the will of God. Paul's criticism of errant Christians was, "You did not so learn Christ." (Ephesians 4:20) Good deeds grow out of our attachment to Christ. Jesus said to his disciples, "I am the vine, you are the branches. He who abides in me, and I in him, he it is that bears much fruit, for apart from me you can do nothing." (John 15:5) *Sanctification*, which means growing in strength to overcome sin and do good deeds, is the work of the Holy Spirit who has united us with Christ.

Life in Christ Means Freedom from the Law

Non-christians always associate living a righteous life with laws. Goodness is simply being law-abiding, obeying the do's and don't's of God and masters. Pharisees and their followers rejected Jesus because they believed they had all the religion they needed in the law of Moses. Many people today admire Christ only because he was the greatest of all law-givers.

In the Bible law is not the solution but the problem. We can only be righteous by being freed from laws. The mission of Christ was to free people from the law of Moses. Christ abolished the law of commandments and ordinances. (Ephesians 2:15) Believers in Chriet are dead to the law. (Romans 7:4-6) The thoroughness with which St. Paul treats this subject indicates how vital it is to Christian faith. See Romans 7 and Galatians 3.

WHAT FREEDOM FROM THE LAW MEANS

First and foremost, freedom from the law means being rid of the false and damnable notion that keeping God's law, which is impossible to begin with, is a way of getting on right terms with God. Failing in this, the law offers no solution for any of people's religious or moral problems.

Freedom from the law further means that Christ has freed his followers from subjection to the requirements of the Mosaic law. They have a new master from whom they learn the will of God regarding their behavior. Christ is now their teacher and Lord. "You have one teacher... you have one master, the Christ." (Matthew 23:8-10) God chose us to be conformed to the image of his Son. (Romans 8:29) Christlikeness is the final goal of all God's saving work. "Beloved, we are God's children now; it does not yet appear what we shall be, but we know that when he appears we shall be like him, for we shall see him as he is." (1 John 3:2) Christians love God and people, not because the Ten Commandments require this but because the new covenant, their life in Christ, does. They do not walk through life with a book of laws and rules. They are led by the Spirit of God. (Romans 8:14) The love of Christ controls them. (2 Corinthians 5:14)

Freedom from the law also means serving God as his loving children and not as slaves. The common motivations for keeping laws are fear of punishment and the hope of a reward. Believers in Christ have no punishment to fear since he bore their punishment. "Christ redeemed us from the curse of the law, having become a curse for us." (Galatians 3:13) There is nothing they can merit by good deeds because in Christ all things are already theirs. (1 Corinthians 3:21-23) Freed from the law we are left with the one and only right reason for avoiding sin and living a righteous life, and that is love. "God's love has been poured into our hearts through the Holy Spirit which has been given to us." (Romans 5:5) "We love, because he first loved us." (1 John 4:19) Without love nothing is good, nothing is right. Read 1 Corinthians 13.

The distinctive things about life under the new covenant are knowing in one's heart what God wants us to do, free and spontaneous obedience, and being sure of God's forgiveness for our failures. "This is the covenant which I will make with the house of Israel after those days, says the Lord: I will put my law within them, and I will write it upon their hearts; and I will be their God, and they shall be my people. And no longer shall each man teach his neighbor and each his brother, saying, 'Know the Lord', for they shall know me, from the least of them to the greatest, says the Lord; for I will forgive their iniquity, and I will remember their sin no more." (Jeremiah 31:33-34) Luther used the following illustration to describe the nature of Christian obedience to the will of God.

Before we were brought to faith in Christ we were prisoners of the law. We lived, as it were, in a dingy prison cell behind barred windows and a locked door with a guard pacing the floor outside. Christ freed us. Do we mean he forced his way in and dragged us out into the open to roam at will? No, he did something far better. He dismissed the guard, unlocked the door and gave us the key. He removed the bars from the windows and let in light and sunshine. He furnished and decorated the cell so that it became a beautiful room in which to live. Now, even though we are free to leave, we love our new dwelling and choose to live in it. So the believer, freed from the law, says with the Psalmist, "I delight to do thy will, O my God." (Psalm 40:8)

The Purpose of the Law

If the law of God is powerless to save us or make us righteous what purpose does it serve? It primarily serves a negative purpose. It serves as a mirror to show us our sins and, consequently, our need for Christ and his forgiveness. "Through the law comes knowledge of sin." (Romans 3:20) The law of God serves as a prosecuting attorney. It accuses and condemns us, rightly insisting that we deserve God's wrath and punishment. This conviction must be brought about in our hearts by the Holy Spirit before we can accept Christ as our Savior.

Law also serves to keep a semblance of order in the world. Fear of punishment is not a God-pleasing motivation but it is relatively effective in curbing crime. "The law is not laid down for the just man, but for the lawless and disobedient, for the ungodly and sinners." (1 Timothy 1:9) A Christian does not need the law to make him or her a law-abiding citizen. Christ did that.

The Christian Approach to the Ten Commandments

In view of all that has been said about the law, in what spirit do we Christians approach the Ten Commandments? We remember that they are part of the old covenant which does not pertain to us. They begin with the words, "I am the Lord your God, who brought you out of the land of Egypt." (Exodus 20:2) This is not the story of our deliverance. We remember that for us righteousness can only be found in Christ. God made him to be "our wisdom, our righteousness and sanctification and redemption." (1 Corinthians 1:30) But we also remember that the Ten Commandments were given by God and are not at variance with what Christ taught. He said, "Think not that I have come to abolish the law and the prophets; I have come not to abolish them but to fulfill them." (Matthew 5:17) We remember that Christlikeness means delighting to do the will of God. He taught us to pray, "Thy will be done." We remember how miserably we fail in this and how desperately we need Christ's forgiveness and help. Having been freed from the law we go back to it again and find that it is not a cruel master but God's servant to lead us to Christ.

LOVE SAYS IT ALL

The first three commandments of the decalog (according to our numbering of the commandments) are summed up in the words, "You shall love the Lord your God with all your heart, and with all your soul, and with all your mind." The last seven commandments are summed up in the words, "You shall love your neighbor as yourself." Jesus said, "On these two commandments depend all the law and the prophets." (Matthew 22:37-40). "Love is the fulfilling of the law." (Romans 13:10)

Luther's explanation of each commandment begins with the words, "We should fear and love God that...." A right relationship with God, which sin destroyed but Christ restored, is the foundation for a righteous life. When we put God first in our affections everything else falls into its proper place.

The First Commandment

You shall have no other gods.

The concern of the First Commandment (see page 131) is the living out of our lives wholly under God. It enjoins putting God first (1) in our fears, (2) our love, and (3) our trust.

1. A right fear of God is not a slavish fear of punishment but rather a deep respect and reverence for God. It is the fear of offending one who is both sublime and gracious. It is saying, "How then can I do this great wickedness and sin against God?" (Genesis 39:9) "The fear of the Lord is hatred of evil." (Proverbs 8:13)

2. The love that God requires of us is the love that he offers us in Christ.

"In this the love of God was made manifest among us, that God sent his only Son into the world, so that we might live through him." (1 John 4:9) We love him because he first loved us. God is both the author and object of our love.

"Whom have I in heaven but thee? And there is nothing upon earth that I desire besides thee. My flesh and my heart may fail, but God is the strength of my heart and my portion for ever." (Psalm 73:25-26)

3. Trust in God means wholeheartedly committing our life to his keeping.

"Cast all your anxieties on him, for he cares about you." (1 Peter 5:7)

"In peace I will both lie down and sleep; for thou alone, O Lord, makest me dwell in safety." (Psalm 4:8) Read also Psalms 91 and 131.

WHAT IS FORBIDDEN

The sin against the First Commandment is idolatry, which means to worship any creature or creation of God as God (Psalm 115) or to put one's trust in a fictitious god. Christless religions are also idolatrous religions. Jesus said, "He who does not honor the Son does not honor the Father who sent him." (John 5:23)

In a wider sense, whatever a man loves or fears most is his or her god. Consequently, cowardice or the fear of people (Proverbs 29:25), sinful covetousness or the love of money (Ephesians 5:5), a servile or doting love for a person (Matthew 10:37), self-centeredness, pride, making the enjoyment of pleasure the aim of life (2 Timothy 3:1-5), worry which reveals lack of trust in God (Matthew 6:24-34) are all forms of idolatry. Finally, every sin dishonors God and is therefore a sin against the First Commandment.

GOD'S JEALOUSY

The First Commandment has an appendix (see page 139) which begins with the words, "I am a jealous God." (Exodus 20:5) God wants us wholly to himself. But his jealousy, different from human jealousy, is unselfish. His sole concern is our happiness. Putting God first is the secret of happiness.

"We call God by that name from the word good (sic), as being an eternal fountain which gushes forth abundantly nothing but what is good, and from which flows forth all that is and is called good—If you have a heart that can expect of him nothing but what is good, especially in want and distress and that, moreover, renounces and forsakes everything that is not of God, then you have the only true God. If, on the contrary, it cleaves to anything else, of which it expects more good and help than of God, and does not take refuge in him, but in adversity flees from him, then you have an idol, another god."

—from Luther's Large Catechism

Our response to the First Commandment must be "Woe is me! Christ forgive and help me."

The Second Commandment

You shall not take the name of the Lord your God in vain.

God's names are God's titles. They describe his nature and his works. Whatever God is or does becomes a name for God. He is called Lord, Creator, Redeemer, the Almighty etc., because he is what these names imply.

God's names stand for him somewhat as the flag stands for the country. Insult the flag and you insult the country.

Jesus taught us to pray that we may keep the Second Commandment in the first petition of the Our Father: "Hallowed be Thy name."

WHAT IS FORBIDDEN

Children of God will repent every evil use of God's name (see page 131) such as:

1. Using God's name in vain or employing it uselessly or carelessly ("My God," "Good Lord," "Jesus Christ" etc.).
2. Blaspheming by speaking evil of God or mocking him.

3. Cursing which means in hatred or anger calling down the punishment of God on someone ("Damn you"). Cursing was punishable by death in the Old Testament. (Leviticus 24:14) It is grossly inconsistent for Christians to use God's name to curse. St. James says of our tongue: "With it we bless the Lord and Father, and with it we curse men, who are made in the likeness of God. From the same mouth come blessing and cursing. My brethren, this ought not to be so." (James 3:9-10)

4. Swearing or calling upon God as a witness when the occasion does not demand or call for it.

    a. Swearing to a lie or perjury. (Leviticus 19:12) For example, St. Peter swearing that he did not know Jesus. (Matthew 26:72)

    b. Swearing to commit sin. (Acts 23:12)

c. Frivolous, thoughtless swearing. (Matthew 5:33-37)

d. Swearing in uncertain things. (Matthew 14:6-9)

Swearing is permissible when an oath is made for the glory of God or, as in court, for the welfare of our neighbor. Christ and Paul swore. (Matthew 26:63-64 and 2 Corinthians 1:23)

5. The performance of superstitious acts, such as conjuring, fortune-telling, consulting the dead, sorcery and witchcraft, as practiced by cults and individuals. The Bible calls these practices an abomination to the Lord (Deuteronomy 18:10-12) and requires Christians to abandon them. (Acts 19:18-19)

6. Lying by God's name. Teaching false doctrine as the word of God.

"Behold I am against the prophets, says the Lord, who use their tongues and say, 'Says the Lord.'" (Jeremiah 23:31)

7. Deceiving by God's name. Covering up one's sinful life with a show of piety (hypocrisy).

"Not everyone who says to me, 'Lord, Lord,' shall enter the kingdom of heaven, but he who does the will of my Father who is in heaven." (Matthew 7:21) "This people honors me with their lips, but their heart is far from me; in vain do they worship me, teaching as doctrines the precepts of men." (Matthew 15:8)

In the next lesson we shall discuss making the proper use of God's name in prayer.

Talking It Over

Use each of the following statements and questions as a basis for discussion.

1. Why is a right relationship with God necessary for a righteous life?

2. —righteousness is Christlikeness

3. —the definition of a good deed

4. What does the New Testament mean by saying that Christ has freed us from the law?

5. —why we still need God's law

6. —a Christian approach to the Ten Commandments

7. How do we commonly break the first two commandments?

True and False Statements

Circle the letter **T** for true statements and the letter **F** for false statements.

T F 1. People do not need any special enlightenment to know what a good deed is.

T F 2. The Ten Commandments were "a way to heaven" for Old Testament believers.

T F 3. For Christians the primary purpose of the law is to show them their sins and lead them to daily repentance.

T F 4. The laws of God enable people to live more righteous lives.

T F 5. The law of Moses is God's universal law for people in all ages.

T F 6. A good Christian will try to keep all the laws of the Bible.

T F 7. What people do is more important than why they do it.

T F 8. The motivation for obedience to God in both the Old and the New Covenant is, "Because he delivered you and made you his people."

T F 9. One should never fear God.

T F 10. Fear of punishment prompts people to do many things that are God-pleasing.

T   F   11. Keeping the First Commandment means keeping all ten of God's commandments.

T   F   12. Idolatry is not common in our country.

T   F   13. Worry is a form of idolatry.

T   F   14. "Love God and do as you please," is a Christian maxim.

T   F   15. A person's god is whatever he or she most loves and desires.

T   F   16. Just as a jealous husband wants his wife all to himself, so God wants us wholly to himself.

T   F   17. All titles, attributes and works of God are included under the names of God.

T   F   18. Every unmeaningful use of God's name is sinful.

T   F   19. Only God has the right to curse.

T   F   20. It is always wrong to swear.

T   F   21. Sorcery was more common in biblical times than it is today.

Bible Reading

The Epistle to the Galatians

A Prayer For Love

O God,
who has prepared for those who love you
such good things as pass human
understanding,
pour into our hearts such love
toward you that we, loving you
above all things,
may obtain your promises,
which exceed all that we can
desire;
through Jesus Christ,
your Son,
our Lord.

10

THE PRAYER LIFE

PREVIEW

Luther's explanation of The Ten Commandments points out not only what they prohibit but also what they enjoin. Our life in Christ is not just a matter of not doing what is wrong or of destroying all the weeds that grow in the garden of the soul. It is a positive power. It is doing what is right or planting seed in the plowed garden. Christ said, "He who abides in me, and I in him, will bear much fruit." (John 15:5)

If there is a wrong use of God's name to be avoided there is also a right use of God's name to be cultivated. Luther says, "Call on him in prayer, praise and thanksgiving." The keeping of the Second Commandment requires a life of prayer.

What is prayer? What is there to pray about? Why and how should we pray? We shall also discuss, on the basis of the Third Commandment, the importance of the word of God for a life of prayer and worship.

What Is Prayer?

In its most limited sense, to pray means to ask something of God (petition). Jesus said, "Ask, and you will receive, that your joy may be full." (John 16:24)

In a wider sense, prayer means holding conversation with God. The church is called "a house of prayer" (Matthew 21:13) because there we hold conversation with God. We speak to him, confessing our sins and offering him our praise and thanksgiving, and he speaks to us, forgiving us and instructing us in the way of life.

This is also the nature of our daily private prayers. It is talking with God (not just to God) which implies listening, too, to what God has to say. It is not only telling God what we want but also and primarily finding out what God wants. Jesus taught us to pray, "Your will be done," and this sums up all that the child of God wants.

God speaks to us through his word which, as we noted earlier, is both a dynamic and teaching word. Christians hear God speaking to them in his acts of providence and judgment which prompt them to pray. God often answers their prayers by doing what they ask. "This poor man cried, and the Lord heard him and saved him out of all his troubles." (Psalm 34:6) The word of God in answer to our prayers is also a word of instruction that comforts, strengthens and gives direction. He speaks to us when, in our joys and sorrows, we call to mind his word and promises. Obviously, the better we know the Bible the better we can pray.

In the widest sense, prayer is the acknowledgment of God in all our ways (Proverbs 3:6), the practice of his presence in our lives, waking or sleeping. It is the companionship of God enjoyed both consciously and subconsciously. Thus St. Paul admonishes Christians to pray constantly to God. (1 Thessalonians 5:16) Prayer life is the life in fellowship with God which Christ restored.

What Is There to Talk About?

Our interest now is in prayer as conversation with God. The topics of conversation are the following:

1. PRAISE AND THANKSGIVING

To praise God means to say how good and wonderful is God. The Psalter, the best of all prayer books, is full of praise to God (e. g., Psalms 96-100).

Every blessing we have received from God is a subject for prayer. Each day there must be new prayers of thanksgiving because his mercies are "new every morning." (Lamentations 3:23) Children of God are always reminding themselves, "Bless the Lord, O my soul, and forget not all his benefits." (Psalm 103:2)

2. CONFESSION

The sins we commit against God and people are also subjects for prayer. As we look back over our day we shall remember not only God's mercies but our lovelessness. Confession is not only good for the soul but necessary for the enjoyment of God's forgiveness.

"If we say we have no sin, we deceive ourselves, and the truth is not in us. If we confess our sins, he is faithful and just, and will forgive our sins and cleanse us from all unrighteousness." (1 John 1:8-9)

3. INTERCESSION OR PRAYING FOR OTHERS

Caring about the needs, sorrows and joys of others is an essential part of Christlikeness which must find expression in our prayers.

"Let each of you look not only to his own interests, but also to the interest of others." (Philippians 2:4)

"First of all, then, I urge that supplications, prayers, intercessions and thanksgivings be made for all men, for kings and all who are in high positions." (1 Timothy 2:1-2)

4. PETITION

By petition we mean asking God for the things we need. Our foremost needs relate to letting God have his way with us. We always need greater faith in him and love for people. Jesus also taught us to pray for our "daily bread" or for our bodily needs. There is no limitation on what we dare ask for in Jesus' name. He promised, "Truly, truly, I say to you, if you ask anything of the Father, he will give it to you in my name." (John 16:23)

Neglect of prayer often explains the emptiness in our lives. "You do not have because you do not ask." (James 4:2)

After the example of our Lord (Luke 22:42), we add to our petitions for bodily needs the words, "If it be your will." Believers are content to leave the final decision of what is best for them with their wise and gracious heavenly Father. He will give us what we ask or something better. Jesus said, "If you then, who are evil, know how to give good gifts to your children, how much more will the heavenly Father give the Holy Spirit to those who ask him!" (Luke 11:13)

Spiritual Requirements of Prayer

1. Prayer must be in the name of Jesus, whether or not his name is mentioned. It is for his sake, who atoned for our sins and reconciled us to God, that God answers our prayers. Prayer requires faith in him as our Mediator and Redeemer.

"Truly, truly, I say to you, if you ask anything of the Father, he will give it to you in my name." (John 16:23)

Praying in the name of Jesus also implies placing one's self within the framework of his life and teachings. There can be no selfish or hateful praying in the name of Jesus.

2. We must pray with confidence, that is, with firm trust that our prayers in Jesus' name will be answered. He said, "Whatever you ask in prayer, you will receive, if you have faith." (Matthew 21:22) This does not mean that we can always be sure that God will give us what we ask. It means we can be sure that he will answer our prayer and that what we receive will be best for us. All petitions to God are subordinate to the prayer, "Your will be done." Sure of God's love, Christians would not want it any other way.

Acknowledging God in All Our Ways

As a Christian hymn puts it, "Prayer is the Christian's vital breath." The apostle admonishes, "Rejoice always, pray constantly, give thanks in all circumstances; for this is the will of God in Christ Jesus for you." (1 Thessalonians 5:16-18) This is not exaggeration. "In him we live and move and have our being." (Acts 17:28) We can not and would not separate him from anything that happens in our life. For all our blessings we owe him our thanks and praise. For all our sins we need his forgiveness. For all our sorrows we need his comfort. For all our weaknesses we need his strength. Praying constantly is acknowledging God in all our ways. (Proverbs 3:6)

But it must also be put into words. There must be daily conversation with God about what is going on in our lives. The danger of thanking God for everything is that we may not really be thanking him for anything. The danger of confessing all our sins is that we may not be confessing any sins. The Christian must cultivate the habit of setting aside fixed times and places for daily prayer. Jesus called the church "a house of prayer." He also urges us to pray in the privacy of our homes. "But when you pray, go into your room and shut the door and pray to your Father who is in secret; and your Father who sees in secret will reward you." (Matthew 6:6)

PRAYER BOOKS

Besides the Bible, prayer books and books of devotion may have an important place in our prayer life. Lutheran hymnals are a rich source for daily devotions. They contain responsive prayers (suffrages) for mornings and other times, daily prayers, Psalms for daily prayer, and a daily lectionary, or readings, from the Bible that correspond to the church year. Prayer books, however, cannot say everything for us. Much of our daily conversation with God will arise from our particular needs and be couched in our own language which God will have no trouble understanding.

MEDITATION

Meditation is a way of acknowledging God in all our ways. The many parables of our Lord grew out of his habit of viewing the physical world as a mirror which reflects God's sovereignty and goodness. He found sermons in blades of grass, lilies of the field, sparrows and in daily life situations. This Christlike practice requires special cultivation in our hectic, noisy world.

Does God Answer Prayer?

What Christians believe about this is summed up in the words: "This is the confidence which we have in him, that if we ask anything according to his will he hears us." (2 John 5:14)

We should not think our prayers are unanswered when nothing changes in the conditions under which we live. God's chief concern is changing us as we grow in Christlikeness. He did not remove the thorn from Paul's flesh but he assured him of his grace. (2 Corinthians 12:7-9) He did not take away the bitter cup from his Son in Gethsemane but he gave him courage and strength to drink it. (Luke 22:39-46) Prayer may or may not lighten our burden but it will strengthen us to carry it. Christians not only pray "give me" but also "make me."

The "Our Father"

The "Our Father," the prayer our Lord taught his disciples, is the model prayer for Christians. It puts God first. Its concern is God's name, God's kingdom, God's will. It does not overlook bodily needs, "our daily bread," which causes us so much anxiety. It teaches us concern for others. There are no "I's" and "me's" in it, but "we" and "us." It asks for God's greatest gifts: forgiveness, deliverance in temptation and from all evil. See Luther's explanation of the "Our Father" on page 134.

The Third Commandment

Remember the Sabbath Day, to keep it holy.

Prayer, as has been pointed out, is talking to God and then listening to what he has to say to us. God speaks to us in the sacred scriptures. The primary concern of our prayers is the will of God. It is in his word that God makes known to us his holy and gracious will.

The Third Commandment, according to Luther's explanation (see page 131), warns against neglecting God's word and teaches us to have a holy regard for it and gladly to hear and learn it.

A LIBERAL INTERPRETATION

It must be observed that Luther exercised a great deal of liberty in his interpretation of the Third Commandment. The words, "Remember the Sabbath Day, to keep it holy," meant that the people of the Old Covenant were to observe Saturday as a day of rest and worship. (Exodus 20:8-11) Christians are not bound by this commandment for the following reasons.

1. Christ freed them from subjection to the Mosaic law, as we noted in a previous discussion. St. Paul says of believers in Christ, "If you are led by the Spirit you are not under the law." (Galatians 5:18)

2. Old Testament ceremonial laws pertaining to the Sabbath, to festivals and holidays, to the offering of sacrifices, and to distinctions between clean and unclean foods are specifically declared to be invalid in the New Testament. "Let no one pass judgment on you in questions of food and drink or with regard to a festival or a new moon or a sabbath. These are only a shadow of what is to come;

but the substance belongs to Christ." (Colossians 2:16-17). Christ is our sabbath. In him is our rest.

No specific days of worship or festival days are commanded in the New Testament. The church observes Sunday as the Lord's Day and festivals such as Christmas, Easter and Pentecost not by divine command but by choice.

The question Luther answers in his explanation of the Third Commandment is, "What does the Spirit of Christ lead us to do?" His answer is, "To be worshipers of God and to love his word."

WHAT IS FORBIDDEN

Christians should not neglect or despise God's word:

1. By ignoring Bible reading and church attendance, or regarding these practices as being of minor importance.

"Let the word of Christ dwell in you richly." (Colossians 3:16) "Not neglecting to meet together [for worship] as is the habit of some." (Hebrews 10:25)

2. By refusing to believe what it teaches.

"The message which they heard did not benefit them, because it did not meet with faith in the hearers." (Hebrews 4:2)

3. By reading and hearing it but not doing what it says.

"Blessed are those who hear the word of God and keep it." (Luke 11:28)

THE WORD OF GOD NOURISHES OUR LIFE IN GOD

As food sustains physical life so the word of God nourishes spiritual life. Starvation means death is a law that recognizes no excuse. Jesus said that it is by the word of God (1) that man lives; (2) that hearing it is the one thing needful; (3) and that hearing it is proof that we are of God.

1. Matthew 4:4—"Man shall not live by bread alone, but by every word that proceeds from the mouth of God."

2. Read Luke 10:38-42.

3. John 8:47—"He who is of God hears the words of God; the reason why you do not hear them is that you are not of God."

THE IMPORTANCE OF CHURCH ATTENDANCE

Public worship is the believers' chief spiritual meal. There they partake of the Lord's Supper. There they feast on the word of God which God has entrusted to the church. The ascended Christ supplies the church with ministers and teachers for the growth and edification of all its members. (Ephesians 4:8-16) Pastors have been given the divine command, "Take heed to yourselves and to all the flock, in which the Holy Spirit has made you overseers, to care for the church of God which he obtained with the blood of his own Son." (Acts 20:28)

Christ, whose followers we are, faithfully attended the Sabbath Day services (Luke 4:16), despite the fact, we may add, that he found much fault with the church in his day and was even persecuted by church people. (Luke 4:28-29)

Christians meeting together for worship and the celebration of the sacraments is taken for granted in the New Testament. Of the early Christians it is said, "Day by day, attending the temple together and breaking bread in their homes, they partook of food with glad and generous hearts, praising God and having favor with all the people. And the Lord added to their number day by day those who were being saved." (Acts 2:46-47)

Jesus promised, "Where two or three are gathered in my name, there am I in the midst of them." (Matthew 18:20)

Psalm 84 expresses the child of God's love for the services of his house.

Talking It Over

Use each of the following questions as a basis for discussion.

1. What is meant by saying that prayer is talking with God?

2. What are the four general subjects of prayer?

3. What is the relation between prayer and faith in Christ?

4. In what sense do Christians pray constantly?

5. What plan shall we follow for a daily period of prayer?

6. How must the question, "Does God answer prayer?" be answered?

7. How does God answer our prayers?

8. Do we understand all the petitions of the "Our Father"?

9. Explain Luther's interpretation of the Third Commandment.

10. What is the relation of the word of God to our life with God?

11. Are we convinced about the importance of church attendance?

True and False Statements

Circle the letter **T** for true statements and the letter **F** for false statements.

T F 1. Prayer simply means talking to God.

T F 2. The person who feels no need for anything has nothing to pray about.

T F 3. We should add, "Your will be done," to every prayer.

T F 4. People who are wholly ignorant of God's word cannot really pray.

T F 5. Praying for others does not help them but it promotes love for others.

T F 6. Our very prayers may reveal how selfish and worldly-minded we are.

T F 7. It is always better to make up one's own prayers than to read prayers from a book.

T   F   8. The biblical admonition to pray constantly was not meant to be taken literally.

T   F   9. Every prayer must be made in the name of Jesus.

T   F 10. God answers our prayers only when he wants to give us what we ask.

T   F 11. We can ask for anything our heart desires as long as we pray in the name of Jesus.

T   F 12. Healing the body is less important to God than healing the soul.

T   F 13. The Third Commandment does not pertain to Christians at all.

T   F 14. The day of worship was changed from Saturday to Sunday in the New Testament.

T   F 15. Private worship of God is more important than participating in public worship.

T   F 16. Jesus found much fault with the services of worship in his day.

T   F 17. Religious broadcasts over radio and television may take the place of going to church.

T   F 18. The Bible takes it for granted that the children of God will meet regularly in public worship.

Bible Reading

The Epistle to the Philippians

The Prayer of St. Francis

THE PRAYER OF ST. FRANCIS

Lord, make me an instrument of your peace,
    Where there is hatred—
    let me sow love.
    Where there is injury—
    let me sow pardon.
    Where there is doubt—faith
            despair—hope
            darkness—light.
    Where there is sadness—joy.

O divine Master, grant that I may not so much seek
    to be consoled as to console;
    to be understood as to understand
    to be loved as to love.

11

LIFE EXPRESSED IN
CORPORATE WORSHIP

PREVIEW

When we come to know God as our Father we look about and see that we have many brothers and sisters in Christ who walk with us and share our hopes and concerns. The child of God is a member of a large family. God made his children in Christ to be dependent on one another. No one in the Christian church ever walks alone. We all need the Christ who serves us through our fellow-believers. We nourish one another. We grow up together "to mature manhood, to the measure of the stature of the fulness of Christ....joined and knit together." (Ephesians 4:13-16) The apostle admonishes, "Let the word of Christ dwell in your richly, teach and admonish one another in all wisdom, and sing psalms and hymns and spiritual songs with thankfulness in your hearts to God." (Colossians 3:16)

This togetherness in Christ finds its fullest expression in the church service. Here the family of God meets in his and their house to unite their prayers and to become increasingly united in their Christian faith and service to God and people.

The Service of Worship

The word *worship* was originally "worthship." In worship we show how much God is worth to us or how precious he is to us. We acknowledge that God is deserving of our trust, our love, our praise and our obedience. More specifically, Christian worship is celebration of God's coming to us and making himself known to us in his Son Jesus Christ, the living Word, and sharing with us the fruits of his death and resurrection.

The public worship of Christians is called a *Service*. Another name for public worship is *Liturgy* which is derived from the Greek word *leitourgia* which means public service. A church service is not just talk. It is transaction. God serves us. He meets with us, forgives us, nourishes and strengthens us, comforts and corrects us and offers us his abiding presence to go with us. We also serve God in worship both in word and deed. In response to his self-giving we offer him our lives with all their talents and powers. We do his will. We practice our love for people in our prayers and offerings.

The Lutheran Church Service

ANCIENT FORMS OF WORSHIP

The Lutheran Church is a liturgical church, which means that it uses ancient and traditional forms of worship. Its major service, in which Holy Communion is celebrated, dates back in large measure to the middle of the fourth century. This service has, in fact, come to be known as The Service. Another common name for it, of Latin origin, is the *Mass*.

LUTHER'S CONTRIBUTION

Luther put the Mass into the language of the people, popularized hymn singing, further involved worshipers in the liturgy by requiring them to take an active part, and eliminated heresies that had crept in.

LUTHERAN BOOKS OF WORSHIP

Unfortunately, not all Lutheran congregations use the same book of worship. Preference is given in this lesson to the widely used "Lutheran Book of Worship" published in 1978. Variations found in different Lutheran books of worship, such as "Lutheran Worship" published in 1982, or others old and new, do not pose any great problem for the study of the Lutheran church service. They do not affect the essential structure of the liturgy that all Lutherans have in common.

THE HIGH IDEALS OF THE SERVICE

Since almost all the words are taken from the word of God, The Service prescribes an ideal worship which we can never attain but never stop trying to attain. It puts into our mouths words of humility, praise and adoration of God, concern and love for people which we may not always feel like saying but which we ought to say. Someone has said, "The Service confronts me with eternal truths and places me upon the everlasting hills. Having worshiped with angels and archangels I can view the problems and worries of daily life with a balanced perspective."

SAMENESS AND VARIATION

There is both sameness and variation in The Service from Sunday to Sunday. There are parts of The Service that are ordinarily used every Sunday and are therefore called the Ordinaries. The parts of The Service that are different from week to week are called Propers. The Propers supply the appropriate (whence the name *Propers*) lessons and prayers, giving to each service a distinctive emphasis relating to our life in Christ.

THE CHURCH YEAR

The liturgical church has its own calendar and its own seasons and holidays relating to the life of Christ. Each Sunday has its own name and its own lessons and prayers (Propers). Year after year the church relives the life of her Lord. The first half of the church year embraces the major events in his life, from his birth to his ascension into heaven and his Pentecostal gift of the Holy Spirit. It is therefore called the festival half of the church year.

The three major festivals are Christmas, Easter and Pentecost. Each designates not just a day but a season. The Christmas season embraces the preparatory season of Advent, which means coming, and refers to the coming of Christ, past, present and future. The church year begins with the first Sunday in Advent. Easter is preceded by the forty days (not counting Sundays) of Lent, ending with Holy Week in which the institution of the Lord's Supper (Maundy Thursday) and the death of Christ (Good Friday) are commemorated. Pentecost celebrates the life-giving work of the Holy Spirit. It is preceded by the Ascension of our Lord, forty days after his resurrection, and is followed by the remaining Sundays of the church year, called Sundays after Pentecost.

The many Sundays after Pentecost comprise the non-festival half of the church year in which the church rehearses the teachings and deeds of her Lord and the workings of the Holy Spirit. It is also known as the season of growth.

SAINTS' DAYS

Another characteristic of liturgical churches is the observance of saints' days. In this connection the word *saints* applies to persons who were outstanding witnesses of Christ. The list is primarily composed of New Testament characters, the apostles of Jesus, John the Baptist, Mary, the mother of Jesus, Mary Magdalene, and Stephen, the first Christian martyr. The Lutheran Book of Worship adds to this list the names of famous post-apostolic men and women whose lives Christians might well choose to commemorate. We do not worship saints, but we honor them, thank God for their lives and learn from them to witness boldly for Christ.

VISUAL AIDS

Liturgical churches commonly use many visual aids to benefit the worshiper. The altar, the focal point of the church, is reverenced as a symbol of God's presence. A crucifix or cross is prominently displayed above the altar to remind us that we owe our life with God to the sacrificial death of Christ. Colored paraments are used to conform to the mood of the season of the church year. The basic liturgical colors are green (for non-festival seasons), white (for festivals), blue (for hope), purple (for penitential seasons) and red (for saints' days, church festivals and parish celebrations). Numerous symbols are used as reminders of the presence, grace and power of God. The vestments of pastors serve to hide their persons and remind worshipers of their priestly and prophetic office. They emphasize that they speak as representatives of the Lord to the church and as representatives of the church to the Lord.

CEREMONY

Ceremony, which for our present purpose means bringing our body into acts of worship, is freely practiced in a liturgical service of worship. Worshipers reverently rise, kneel, bow their heads and make the sign of the cross. These traditional Christian practices indicate a desire to worship God with body and soul, and also to let people know that we are not ashamed of what we believe. Imagine cheering a football team without using your body.

Explanation of The Service

Deriving benefit from participation in a liturgical service of worship requires, besides practice, preparation and study. The following explanation of The Service is intended to serve this purpose.

COMMUNION WITH GOD

The Service is communion with God. He speaks words and things to us. We speak to him with words and actions. The former is called the sacramental part of The Service, and the latter the sacrificial part.

THE SACRAMENTAL PARTS OF THE SERVICE

The Service may begin with the public confession of sins followed by God's word of forgiveness. The good news of forgiveness, which makes communion with him possible for us sinners, is the chief message of The Service.

THE LESSONS FROM THE WORD OF GOD   Three lessons are read in The Service, one usually from the Old Testament, one from the letters of the apostles (the Epistle) and a narrative from the life of our Lord (the Gospel). The Gospel is a high point in The Service. It normally sets the theme which influences the prayers, hymns and the sermon.

THE SERMON   The purpose of the sermon is to establish the connection between the message of the lessons and the worshiper's daily life. The premise of every Christian sermon is that the all-embracing problem of people is sin, which needs to be repented of and for which Christ alone has the happy solution.

HOLY COMMUNION   In the sacrament of Holy Communion, God wraps up all his precious gifts and offers them to us in a single package. The gift is Christ, his Son, who with the bread and wine, offers us his body and blood, given and shed for our forgiveness, salvation and life.

THE SACRIFICIAL PARTS OF THE SERVICE

The actions of the worshipers can be summed up in the word *ACTS* — Adoration, Confession, Thanksgiving, Supplication. These words may serve as an outline for our private prayers as well as a church service.

THE INVOCATION AND GREETING   The Service may begin with the words, "In the name of the Father, and of the Son, and of the Holy Spirit." They are called the Invocation because they invoke (call in) God's presence. The "Amen" with which Christians respond to prayers spoken by others, means so be it. It is the worshiper's way of saying "Me, too."

The Service may also begin with the minister's greeting, "The grace of the Lord Jesus Christ the love of God and the fellowship of the Holy Spirit be with you all" (2 Corinthians 13:14), to which the congregation responds, "And also with you." This is an expression of mutual loving concern that is essential to Christian worship.

THE KYRIE   Kyrie is the Greek word for Lord. "Lord, have mercy" was the prayer of blind men (Matthew 9:27), lepers (Luke 17:12-13) and others who begged our Lord to heal them. The Kyrie is an ardent cry for help, not only for ourselves and our congregation, but for the whole church and the world. It is a cry to God out of the depths.

THE HYMN OF PRAISE   In a swift change of mood the congregation now sings a hymn of praise to God who answered every cry of distress by sending his Son to be the Savior of the world. In him we have forgiveness, peace and victory over all the forces of evil.

THE SALUTATION   The mutual greeting, "The Lord be with you," occurs several times in The Service as preparation for what follows. In this case it means, "While we pray and listen to the word of God."

THE PRAYER FOR THE DAY   For each Sunday and festival the church has appointed a special short prayer to be read. Both the practice and many of these prayers themselves, originally of one sentence, are ancient. The Collect, as it is called, is a prayerful response to the thought of the day or season of the church year. It sums up (collects) and expresses in a few words the prayers of all the worshipers.

RESPONSE TO THE LESSONS AND SERMON   The lessons and sermon are God's word to us. But they call for a response. Our Lord said, "Blessed rather are those who hear the word of God and keep it." (Luke 11:28) We are admonished to "receive with meekness the implanted word, which is able to save your souls." (James 1:21) Believers let the word of God shape their lives, like clay in the potter's hands.

The congregation responds to the Epistle with an "Alleluia!" We praise God for his scoldings as well as his words of comfort. It respectfully rises for the reading of the Gospel and expresses its adoration for Christ with short outbursts of praise before and after it is read. A fruitful hearing of the word of God requires a spirit of humility, reverence and thankfulness.

THE CREED   After singing the hymn of the day, the congregation prayerfully recites the Nicene or the Apostles' Creed. The creed is the worshipers' response to the word of God that was read and preached. They say, "I believe." It is an appropriate expression of faith because it embraces the fundamental beliefs of Christians. It mentions the big truths which they all hold in common and that are their bond of union. Worshipers pray the creed in the sense that they recognize their need for greater trust in God, as Creator, Savior and Life-giver. The Nicene Creed is used in all festival services; the Apostles' Creed at other times.

THE PRAYERS   The chief characteristics of the prayers of the church are thanksgiving to God for his manifold goodness and intercessions for people. They reflect God's loving concern for all people. No sufferer, no need in the church or in society, is willfully overlooked. Members of the congregation are encouraged to request prayers of thanksgiving or intercession for relatives and friends.

THE PEACE GREETING   At this point in The Service (or after the "Our Father" in some orders), the minister greets the congregation with the words, "The peace of the Lord be with you." Worshipers may then greet one another with the same words. In the New Testament church worshipers greeted one another with a kiss. (Romans 16:16)

THE OFFERING   In the early church, worshipers brought with them food and other gifts for the poor and the clergy, also the bread and wine for Holy Communion. During the singing of a psalm they came forward and placed their gifts on or near the altar. The church today has retained the essential features of this ancient practice. A hymn is sung and the offerings of the congregation are gathered and brought to the altar and offered to God in prayer. Our gifts of money betoken the giving of ourselves to God.

THE GREAT THANKSGIVING   The minister's greeting, "The Lord be with you," now introduces the climactic part of The Service, the partaking of the Lord's Supper. Worshipers are admonished to lift up their hearts, to be "uphearted" and not downhearted, and to give thanks to the Lord. The first subject of thanksgiving, called The Preface, relates to the good news of the particular day or season of the church year. Thereupon follows one of the most ancient Christian hymns, the "Holy, Holy, Holy." The first part is from the Old Testament. (Isaiah 6:3) They are the words which the great prophet, in a vision, heard from the lips of an angel. The second part is from the New Testament. (Matthew 21:9) These are the words of welcome with which the people of Jerusalem greeted Jesus on Palm Sunday. With them we open our hearts to Christ who is coming to us in the blessed sacrament. *Hosanna* means "Save, now."

THE WORDS OF INSTITUTION   A very significant part of The Service is the reading of the biblical words telling us what our Lord said and did when he instituted the sacrament of Holy Communion. (1 Corinthians 11:23-26) They are the word of God which makes Holy Communion a sacrament and gives it saving power. They remind us of our Lord's command, his presence and his forgiveness.

The words of institution may be incorporated in a prayer in which worshipers thank God for the salvation he promised and offers in Christ, and pray for faith to receive him. Our Lord gave thanks before he gave the bread to his disciples. (I Corinthians 11:24)

The Great Thanksgiving concludes with a hymn of adoration, the "Our Father" (the family prayer before the family meal), and the gathering at the table.

The Service ends with a hymn, a short prayer and the blessing of God.

Minor Services

Besides the major service, various minor church services are held. One is an abbreviated form of The Service in which Holy Communion is not celebrated. Other minor services for all days of the week are Matins (a morning service), Vespers (an evening service), and Compline (for the close of the day). These services may be used by families and groups in their homes or wherever they may be.

Talking It Over

Use each of the following statements and questions as a basis for discussion.

1. —the significance of calling public worship a Service

2. —distinctive features of a liturgical service

3. What is meant by Ordinaries and Propers?

4. What are the main parts of the church year?

5. —the reason for visual aids and ceremony in services of worship

6. What are the sacramental parts of The Service?

7. What are the sacrificial parts of The Service?

8. Why should partaking of the Lord's Supper be regarded as the climax of The Service?

9. What may be listed under minor services?

True and False Statements

Circle the letter **T** for true statements and the letter **F** for false statements.

T F 1. Talking and listening to God fully describe what takes place in a church service.

T F 2. "I didn't get anything out of The Service," is a common justifiable complaint.

T F 3. Newcomers are apt to feel lost in a liturgical service.

T F 4. The sermon is the most important part of The Service.

T F 5. The chief reason for going to church is to learn the word of God.

T F 6. It is largely true that we get out of a church service what we put into it.

T F 7. The chief feature of a liturgical service are ritual and ceremony.

T F 8. Forms of worship are prescribed in the New Testament.

T   F   9. Martin Luther wrote a new liturgy for the Lutheran Church.

T   F   10. The traditional service should never be tampered with.

T   F   11. The weekly repetition of parts of The Service makes worship difficult for most people.

T   F   12. The church year begins on January 1st.

T   F   13. Year after year the church in her worship relives the life of the Lord.

T   F   14. There are no saints' days on the Lutheran church calendar.

T   F   15. Liturgical churches like to make use of visual aids in their worship.

T   F   16. Worshiping God is a spiritual act which does not require the use of the body.

T   F   17. The Service is a transaction between God and worshipers which lasts for about one hour.

For Further Study

In evaluating a sermon, arrange the following words in the order of their importance.

_____ Instructive

_____ Interesting

_____ Inspiring

_____ Scriptural

_____ Christ-centered

Bible Reading

The Book of Psalms
Psalm 90-107

A Worshiper's Prayer

Holy Spirit,
Lord and giver of life,
     shed abroad your life-giving
     spirit in our hearts.
Give us grace to receive your word meekly
and to bring forth fruit with patience.
        Be with all who minister in your word
        and sacrament, so that we, together with
        them and all who worship with us,
        may have life and have it abundantly;
through Jesus Christ our Lord.

12

LIFE EXPRESSED IN LOVE

FOR PEOPLE

PREVIEW

With a few digressions we have concluded our Christian interpretation of the first table of the Mosaic law which requires loving God above all else. "This," our Lord said, "is the great and first commandment." But He immediately went on to say that the second, namely, "You shall love your neighbor as yourself," is like it. (Matthew 22:36-40) Love for God and love for people are of the same cloth. Love for God not only requires but also generates love for people. "He who does not love does not know God; for God is love." (1 John 4:8) The proof that we are alive, in the Biblical sense, is in the love we have for people. "We know that we have passed out of death into life, because we love the brethren. He who does not love abides in death." (1 John 3:14) Without love, religious talk, knowledge, faith and zeal are all sham. (1 Corinthians 13:1-3)

A study of the second table of the Mosaic law, in the light of its fulfillment in Christ, will help us to apply the royal law of love to specific areas and problems of life.

What Is Love?

The word love, with all of its self-centered and romantic overtones and undertones, can scarcely serve to describe the feeling for people which reflects God's feeling for them. We have something better than a word. We have a living picture in Christ. "This is my commandment," he said, "that you love one another as I have loved you. Greater love has no man than this, that a man lay down his life for his friends." (John 15: 12-13) "Walk in love," St. Paul admonishes, "as Christ loved us and gave himself up for us." (Ephesians 5:2)

Christ's love for people has qualities which distinguish it from human love. Divine love, which he personifies and shares with us, generates its own power. God loves because it is his nature to love. His love is not response or reaction to lovableness. It embraces the unlovable. "Perhaps for a good man one will dare even to die. But God shows his love for us in that while we were yet sinners Christ died for us." (Roman 5:7-8) God's love is infinite in its outreach as well as its "downreach." It extends to all people. It reveals itself in acts of self-giving. "God so loved the world that he gave his only Son." (John 3:16)

This is the love which Christian love reflects. It loves even when it disapproves. It "covers a multitude of sins." (1 Peter 4:8) It regards everyone in need as a neighbor who must be helped, regardless of his or her race, color or animosities. It rules out prejudice. It recognizes no boundaries or limitations. Read the parable of the Good Samaritan. (Luke 10:25-37)

The Fourth Commandment

Honor your father and your mother.

THE DUTIES OF CHILDREN

As is said of charity, love begins at home. The Fourth Commandment is concerned about the practice of love on our first and nearest neighbors, father and mother. Children should love and respect their parents through whom God has given them life and provides for them (see page 131). After the example of the boy Jesus (Luke 2:51-52) they should willingly serve and obey them.

THE DUTIES OF PARENTS

The manner in which Christian parents bring up their children is determined by their acknowledgment of God's claim on them as their Creator, Redeemer and Lord. Parents are God's stewards, dealing with his precious possessions, and may not do with them as they please but should do as he wills.

This implies a concern about the kinds of growth the Christ-child enjoyed of whom it is said, "Jesus increased in wisdom and in stature, and in favor with God and man." (Luke 2:52)

The word of God places the responsibility of giving children a Christian training chiefly on parents. The apostle admonishes, "Fathers, do not provoke your children to anger, but bring them up in the discipline and instruction of the Lord." (Ephesians 6:4) The home is the best place to learn about the blessedness of life with God, and the example of parents is the best teacher.

Christian parents will also support and make use of the church's schools, not as substitutes for Christian home training, but as valuable aids.

The Christian's Daily Life

By adding the word *masters* to parents in his explanation of the Fourth Commandment, Luther broadened the scope of the commandment to include a Christian attitude toward all rightly constituted authority. Living under God determines how we live as citizens and workers.

CHRISTIAN CITIZENS

Christians regard their political government as God's servant, ordained by him for their good. It is in obedience to God that they pay taxes and obey the laws of the state. Read Romans 13:1-7. When there is a conflict between civil law and the will of God they are bound to say, "We must obey God rather than men." (Acts 5:29) More, however, than obedience is required of Christians who live in a democracy. They have the freedom and responsibility to take an active part in the shaping of a just and humanitarian government. Separation of church and state does not mean surrendering politics to the devil.

As children of God "who so loved the world that he gave his only Son," Christians care when people anywhere suffer in body or spirit. As the salt of the earth, as Jesus said of them, they seek solutions to world problems of human rights, hunger and the unequal distribution of wealth.

THE CHRISTIAN AT WORK

Read Ephesians 6:5-9. St. Paul's reminder to Christian masters and slaves in his day basically applies to Christian employers and employees today. Christ is master of both, and this determines the quality of their behavior. Service rendered to employers, who may be hard to please (1 Peter 2:18), is service rendered to our Lord, and will therefore be distinguished by honesty and trustworthiness. Christian employers should remember that they serve the same Lord, and practice on their employees the justice and kindness they have learned from him.

The Fifth Commandment

You shall not kill.

THE SACREDNESS OF HUMAN LIFE

Every article of our Christian faith teaches the sacredness of human life. God created it, rescued it from sin, through Christ's taking it on and offering it up, and hallows it through his Spirit who makes a person's body his temple. (1 Corinthians 6:19-20) Any deed or word which destroys, shortens or embitters a person's life violates the sacredness of life. "You shall not kill" also applies to suicide and manslaughter (killing through carelessness, e.g., reckless or drunken automobile driving).

The apostle John calls hatred murder (1 John 3:15) because hatred is implicitly the desire to kill. Our Lord regarded being angry with your neighbors, insulting them and calling them fools as violations of the Fifth Commandment. (Matthew 5:21-22)

THE DUTY OF THE STATE TO PRESERVE LIFE

The New Testament recognizes the right of a political government to wield a sword for the purpose of punishing the wrongdoer. (Romans 13:4) Capital punishment is neither commanded nor prohibited. Killing in self-defense or in the defense of others is justifiable only on the grounds that it is necessary for the preservation of life. Wars of aggression are mass murders. The practical difficulty is that pointing out the aggressor is often a matter of choosing between shades of grey.

LOVE FOR PEOPLE

Christian love requires that instead of hurting our neighbors we help them in all their physical needs (see page 140). We are not to act the part of the robber in our Lord's parable of the Good Samaritan. (Luke 10:25-37) The robber's philosophy was, "What is yours is mine; I'll take it." Neither are we to act the part of the Levite and priest who said, "What is mine is mine; I'll keep it." Our philosophy should be that of the Good Samaritan who said, "What is mine is yours; I'll share it." "Be kind to one another, tenderhearted, forgiving one another, as God in Christ forgave you." (Ephesians 4:32) The believer sees Christ in every person who is in need. (Matthew 25:34-40) Reconciliation with God requires seeking reconciliation with people with whom we have quarreled. (Matthew 5:23-26) Christians must be willing to suffer injustice rather than to seek revenge. (Matthew 5:38-39) The weapon with which evil must be overcome is goodness. (Romans 12:19-21)

The Sixth Commandment

You shall not commit adultery.

MARITAL LIFE

Marriage was instituted by God. Eve was created from Adam's side for mutual companionship and for a union of the flesh which made them.partners with God in his work of creation. (Genesis 1:27-28; 2:18-25) Our Lord put his blessing on marriage by attending the wedding at Cana and performing his first miracle to enhance the celebration. (John 2:1-11)

Marital life has its model in the relationship which exists between Christ and his church. Husbands are required to love their wives "as Christ loved the church and gave himself up for her." Wives should love and serve their husbands as the church serves Christ. This is no special subordination because Christians are all subject to one another. Read Ephesians 5:21-25.

As far as the Bible is concerned, a man and woman may be married without a license from the state or a wedding ceremony. What is required for marriage, or living together, is an unconditional commitment on the part of both to a lifelong union.

"UNTIL DEATH US DO PART"

A person never has the right to break a marriage. "What therefore God has joined together, let not man put asunder." (Matthew 19:6) Marriage is dissolved through unrepented acts of adultery or malicious desertion which occurs in different forms. (Matthew 19:9 and 1 Corinthians 7:15)

In such cases the innocent party may request the court to recognize that the marriage has been dissolved. Here, too, as with war, the problem is assigning guilt to one party and innocence to the other. Civil law may regard selfish reasons as grounds for a divorce but the word of God never does. Christians must strive to solve their marital problems with the law of Christian love which "bears all things, believes all things, hopes all things, endures all things." (1 Corinthians 13:7) (See page 132.)

Jesus made the following stringent pronouncements about divorce. A man who divorces his wife, except for unchastity, commits adultery if he marries another. (Matthew 19:9) A man who marries a divorced woman commits adultery. (Matthew 5:32) A woman who divorces her husband commits adultery if she marries another. (Mark 10:12) Yet Jesus always left room for repentance, saying that harlots precede the elders of the people into the kingdom of God (Matthew 21:31) and treating a woman taken in adultery with great compassion. (John 8:3)

THE IDEAL SEXUAL RELATIONSHIP

People's sexual desires, like hunger and thirst, are God-given. It is only their abuse that is sinful. They may be and must be gratified in a manner that is in keeping with the purpose for which he created them. "Let marriage be held in honor among all, and let the marriage bed be undefiled." (Hebrews 13:4)

Christians properly regard sexual union as the sacrament of marriage. It is the physical expression of a spiritual God-ordained union, the two becoming one. (Genesis 2:24) The faith of Christians in the Triune God gives them three urgent reasons for avoiding adultery. God the Father created their body, Christ redeemed it and the Holy Spirit makes it his dwelling place. "Do you not know that your body is a temple of the Holy Spirit within you, which you have from God? You are not your own; you were bought with a price. So glorify God in your body." (1 Corinthians 6:19-20)

OUR SPIRITUAL WEAPONS

The God-implanted desire for purity in matters of sex, as in everything else, involves us in a battle against powerful enemies: the devil, the godless world in which we live and are prone to imitate, and the passions of our flesh which resent being tamed. The only effective weapons in this battle are the word of God and prayer through which God the Savior becomes our ally. "Greater is he that is with us than all they that are against us."

The Seventh Commandment

You shall not steal.

RESPECT FOR OUR NEIGHBOR'S PROPERTY

The Seventh Commandment deals with respect for property. It prohibits taking from our neighbors what belongs to them, whether by force (robbery), or by stealing, or by overcharging, or by underpaying employees, or by not doing an honest day's work, or by any of numerous fraudulent practices (see page 132).

How widespread sins against the Seventh Commandment are may be learned from daily news reports. Less publicized than the sins of people against society, but equally widespread, are the sins of society, or the economic system, against poor and disenfranchised people. It is especially the exploitation of the poor that the biblical prophets unite their voices in condemning.

So far from taking what belongs to others, the Christian will "help them to improve and protect their property and means of making a living." The Golden Rule applies here: "Whatever you wish that men would do to you, do so to them." (Matthew 7:12)

CHRISTIAN STEWARDSHIP

Christians regard their possessions as God's property to be used not as they will but as God directs. It is God's will that they be guided by the law of Christian love in the use they make of their possessions. With them they are bound to provide for their family, to help those in need and to share their Christ with people by making generous financial contributions to the work of the church.

The Eighth Commandment

You shall not bear false witness against your neighbor.

GUARDING OUR NEIGHBOR'S REPUTATION

The Eighth Commandment seeks to guard a person's reputation and to keep relationships between people from breaking up. It forbids gossip, slander and lying about others. Christian love requires defending one's neighbors against gossip and slander, speaking well of them and making charitable judgments of their actions (see page 132). Love believes all good things about one's neighbors and hopes all good things for them. (1 Corinthians 13:7)

slander, speaking well of them and making charitable judgments of their actions (see page 140). Love believes all good things about one's neighbors and hopes all good things for them. (1 Corinthians 13:7)

CONSTRUCTIVE CRITICISM

Christians should admonish one another (Colossians 3:16), speak privately to the person who sins against them (Matthew 18:15-17), and seek to restore a person who has grievously sinned, "in a spirit of gentleness." (Galatians 6:1) They must also know in what spirit criticism must be received. The proper response to criticism is to say sincerely, "Thank you."

The Ninth and Tenth Commandments

You shall not covet your neighbor's house.

You shall not covet your neighbor's wife, or his manservant, or his maidservant, or his cattle, or anything that is your neighbor's.

The word *covet* means earnestly to desire. The apostle admonished us earnestly to desire the higher gifts, above all, Christian love. (1 Corinthians 12:31) The Ninth and Tenth Commandments forbid enviously coveting our neighbor's possessions (see page 132), which implies a lack of love. They compel us to distinguish between legitimate profit making and greed. Sinful covetousness is idolatry (Colossians 3:5) because it regards the possession of things to be the highest good in life.

The Ninth and Tenth Commandments emphasize that God is concerned about what goes on in our hearts. Jesus said, "Out of the heart comes evil thoughts, murder, adultery, fornication, theft, false witness, slander." (Matthew 15:19)

Contentment with what God has given us rules out sinful covetousness and is the secret of happiness. "There is great gain in godliness with contentment; for we brought nothing into the world, and we can not take anything out of the world; but if we have food and clothing, with these we shall be content. But those who desire to be rich fall into temptation, into a snare, into many senseless and hurtful desires that plunge men into ruin and destruction. For the love of money is the root of all evils; it is through this craving that some have wandered away from the faith and pierced their hearts with many pangs." (1 Timothy 6:6-10)

Talking It Over

Use each of the following statements and questions as a basis for discussion.

1. What characterizes Christian love?

2. What distinguishes (1) a Christian home, (2) a Christian citizen, (3) a Christian worker?

3. —what the Fifth Commandment prohibits and enjoins from the Christian point of view

4. —the Christian view of marriage, marital love and sexual desires

5. What are some common business practices which the Seventh Commandment condemns?

6. —what it means to manage one's possessions as God's steward

7. How can we guard our neighbor's reputation?

8. —why God cares about what goes on in our hearts

9. What are the opposites of sinful covetousness?

True and False Statements

Circle the letter **T** for true statements and the letter **F** for false statements.

T   F   1. Loving God is more important and necessary than loving people.

T   F   2. There is nothing Christian about romantic love.

T   F   3. People we love must be worthy of our love.

T   F   4. Even God's love recognizes some boundaries and limitations.

T   F   5. Children are required to love and respect parents who often mistreat them.

T   F   6. Children should be left to decide in later life whether or not they want to attend church.

T   F   7. The most effective religious education of children can be accomplished in the church.

T F   8. A Christian has only one master, the Lord Jesus Christ.

T F   9. Most people keep the Fifth Commandment.

T F 10. There is a Christian way of driving an automobile.

T F 11. All taking of life is murder.

T F 12. Only God has the right to take revenge.

T F 13. Laws of the state regarding divorce are Christian.

T F 14. A Christian should not marry a non-Christian.

T F 15. Sexual desires are a result of human sinfulness.

T F 16. Sexual desires are different from hunger and thirst in some ways.

T F 17. Sexual union is permissible when two people love each other.

T F 18. "It pays to be honest" is a Christian maxim.

T F 19. The Golden Rule is impractical for conducting one's business.

T F 20. Talking about others is permissible as long as we keep within the bounds of truth.

T F 21. We should sometimes speak to others about their faults.

T F 22. It is always right to thank the person who criticizes you.

T F 23. There are no civil laws that prohibit sinful coveting.

T F 24. Coveting is sinful only when it leads to stealing.

T F 25. The measure of people's contentment is a measure of their happiness.

For Further Study

At least one-third of our Lord's teachings related to the use we make of our gifts and talents. On the basis of Matthew 25:14-30, what is wrong with these two common sayings:

- I can do as I please with what is mine.
- Nothing I can do will make any difference.

Bible Reading

The Gospel of Matthew
Chapters 5-7

The First Epistle of John.

A Prayer for the Practice of Love

O God of love,
who has given us a new commandment through your Son,
that we should love one another
as you loved us
and gave your Son for our life, give us,
your children,
a forgiving spirit,
sincere thoughts and a heart to love people;
for the sake of Jesus Christ,
your Son,
our Lord.

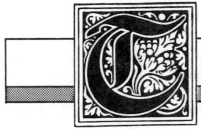

THE CHURCH —

THE COMMUNITY OF THE LIVING

13

PREVIEW

A common saying in our day is, "I can be a Christian without being a member of the church." Can you? What is the church? Who created it? Who are its members? In the face of denominational factions does it have any real unity? What is its work? Does being a member of the church mean being a member of a Christian congregation? On what basis should people choose the congregation they will join? These are some of the questions we shall now discuss in the light of New Testament teaching.

What Is the Church?

The word *church* may mean a building for Christian worship. But the word is never used in this sense in the New Testament because the first century Christians had no church buildings.

Church is also used today in the sense of a denomination (e.g., Lutheran or Roman Catholic Church) but this use is also foreign to the New Testament because the early Christian church was not divided into denominations.

In its primary biblical sense, church means the Christian community, the sum total of people who accept Jesus as their Savior, are baptized and have received the forgiveness of sins and the gift of the Holy Spirit. "Peter said to them, 'Repent, and be baptized every one of you in the name of Jesus Christ for the forgiveness of your sins; and you shall receive the gift of the Holy Spirit. For the promise is to you and your children and to all that are far off, every one whom the Lord our God calls to him.'" (Acts 2:38-39)

It is called "the church of the living God" (1 Timothy 3:15) because it is God's creation and the "church of the Lord" because the Lord Jesus obtained it with his own blood. (Acts 20, 28)

OTHER NAMES FOR CHURCH

Numerous other words are used in the New Testament which bring to light the manifold blessings and privileges which the church enjoys. Our Lord called it the flock (Matthew 26:31), over which he is the shepherd, and the little flock (Luke 12:32) to emphasize that it has greater things to glory in than numerical strength and worldly power. The church is called the bride of Christ. He is her husband and savior who loves and cares for her, and she loves and serves him as a faithful wife. (Ephesians 5:22-32) St. Paul also calls the church the body of Christ of which he is the head and in which all the members are coordinated for service as in a healthy human body. (1 Corinthians 12:12-27) By calling the church "a chosen race, a royal priesthood, a holy nation, God's own people" (1 Peter 2:9), and "Abraham's offspring" (Galatians 3:29) the apostles establish the necessary link between the Christian church and the Old Testament people of God. In the language of St. John the church is the fellowship of living people who have fellowship with the Father and with his Son Jesus Christ. "That which we have seen and heard we proclaim also to you, so that you may have fellowship with us; and our fellowship is with the Father and with his Son Jesus Christ." (1 John 1:3)

"WE BELIEVE IN THE HOLY CHRISTIAN CHURCH"

To say, "We believe in God the Father, in Jesus Christ, his Son, and in the Holy Spirit," requires going on to say, as we do in the Apostles' Creed, "We believe in the holy Christian church." According to Luther's explanation of the Third Article (page 134) we are bound to recognize that what God has done for us, to make us members of the church, he has done for many others with whom we are now united "in the one true faith."

The church is holy, a communion of saints, not because its members are without sin but because they enjoy the forgiveness of Christ, and God's holy word and sacraments through which the Holy Spirit continually sanctifies them, that is, purifies them and empowers them for godly service.

The original term "catholic church," meaning universal church, was later changed in some circles to "Christian church."

CHURCH IN THE SENSE OF A CHRISTIAN CONGREGATION

The word *church* is also used in the New Testament in the sense of a local Christian community or congregation (the church at Rome, Corinth, etc.), the people in a given place who believe in, worship and serve Christ. Although communities of believers in Christ are separated by space and time, "the saints on earth and those above but one communion make."

The Divine—Human Church

The church is divine, bears the nature of God, (1) because it is the shoot of God's planting and the work of his hands (Isaiah 60:21); (2) because it uses tools that were forged by God, his word and sacraments which he has committed to it (Matthew 28:18-20) and through which he works salvation (Romans 1:16); (3) because it enjoys God's protection (Jesus said, "I will build my church, and the powers of death shall not prevail against it."—Matthew 16:18); (4) because it is the temple of the Lord and the dwelling place of God in the Spirit, "built upon the foundation of the apostles and prophets, Christ Jesus himself being the chief cornerstone." (Ephesians 2:20)

The church has a human nature. It is composed of people who, although they are saints in the eyes of God, are still in the flesh. It wears the blemishes of all the imperfections of its members. The church on earth is the militant church still engaged in the fierce battle against the devil, the ungodly world and sinful flesh.

THE CHURCH'S UNITY AND DISUNITY

The divine nature of the church gives it unity; the human nature accounts for its disunity. As saints who are holy before God all members of the church are one in Christ. "There is one body and one Spirit, just as you were called to the one hope that belongs to your call, one Lord, one faith, one baptism, one God and Father of us all, who is above all and through all and in all." (Ephesians 4:4-6) This unity, created by God, is hidden beneath the broken surface of denominationalism and sectarianism brought about by the imperfections of church members who are still in the flesh. Christians experience their God-ordained oneness in the measure in which they act like Christians, just as husband and wife need only act consistently with the fact that God united them in wedlock.

The church on earth will always be the militant church fighting, above all, the battle against its own pride, self-righteousness and lovelessness. There is no greater disrupter of unity in the church than pharisaism, which is forgetting that we sinners are our own worst enemies. Christian unity is maintained by the practice of humility and tolerance. St. Paul begs Christians, "lead a life worthy of the calling to which you have been called, with all lowliness and meekness, with patience, forbearing one another in love, eager to maintain the unity of the Spirit in the bond of peace." (Ephesians 4:1-3) Our Lord prayed that his followers "may all be one; even as thou, Father, art in me, and I in thee." (John 17:21)

The Concerns of the Church

What does God want to accomplish in and through the church? Three things: (1) inner growth in Christlikeness, (2) outward growth in numbers and (3) loving service to humanity.

1. St. Paul in Ephesians 4, 12-13 described the inner growth in the church in terms of "building up the body of Christ, until we all attain to the unity of faith and to

the knowledge of the Son of God, to mature manhood, to the measure of the stature of the fulness of Christ." Through the word of God with which we teach and admonish one another, the sacrament of Holy Communion, and a life of prayer the Holy Spirit, as Luther says, "sanctifies us in the faith," by stages and degrees makes us more Christlike. This inner growth of the church as it affects all of its members describes a major objective of the fellowship of Christians in their worship, teaching and work. The question in the church is not just, "What is being done?", but "What is being done for God's people to further their growth in Christlikeness?"

2. A second major concern of the church is its outward growth, the Lord adding to their number. (Acts 2:47). Members of the church are eager to share their blessings in Christ with people who have no hope and are without God. (Ephesians 2:12) By witnessing for Christ in their daily lives, inviting others to share in their blessed fellowship and supporting the work of their congregation with their gifts and prayers, church members carry on home mission work. They are equally concerned about Christian missions in foreign lands which they establish and support by their offerings and prayers. The Lord of the church directs them to "go and make disciples of all nations." (Matthew 28:19)

3. The church dare never forget that it is the creation and servant of God who "so loved the world that he gave his only Son." (John 3:16) It is the body of Christ through which he ministers to people in all their needs. It sees people through his eyes, hears their complaints with his ears, speaks his words to them and heals them with the touch of his hands. Showing concern for the neglected, the ill-treated, the disenfranchised and the hungry is Christlike work. What we do to these we do to him. "Truly, I say to you, as you did it to one of the least of these my brethren, you did it to me." (Matthew 25:40)

NO SALVATION OUTSIDE THE CHURCH

No, you cannot be a Christian without being a member of the church. Those whom the Lord saves he adds to the church. (Acts 2:47) The church has his word and sacraments through which he accomplishes his life-giving work. The Lord has given to the church the authority to forgive sins. (See "The Office of the Keys" page 138.) People enter into fellowship with God and Christ by entering into fellowship with those who handle the word of life. (1 John 1:1-3) The Bible written by church people for church people, everywhere takes church membership for granted.

The Christian Congregation

The believers' experiential association with the church is through a Christian congregation in their community, the local headquarters of the church. The fellowship of Christians is realized and practiced by groups of Christ's people who have banded themselves together for the worship and service of their Lord. Consequently, the New Testament takes for granted that the members of Christ's body are members of a Christian congregation. A large part of the New Testament is composed of letters written by the apostles to congregations which they had established. They assume that the Christians at Rome, Corinth, etc. were members of the congregations in these cities.

WHY A CHRISTIAN JOINS A CONGREGATION

Believers will want to be faithful members of a Christian congregation so that they might both serve and be served. Our Lord admonished us to listen to the word of God and to teach it, to receive the sacraments and to share them with others. Every aspect of life in a Christian congregation is a taking and giving. If a congregation might be compared to a restaurant then its members are the co-owners and waiters as well as the customers. They eat of the table they have set for others.

The Christian seeks the association of other Christians for mutual edification. Giving and receiving correction, instruction, encouragement and comfort, which membership in a Christian congregation requires, are essential to Christian life. None of us in the church can "go it alone." The fire in an ember set apart from other embers loses its glow.

"Bear one another's burdens, and so fulfill the law of Christ." (Galatians 6:2)

"Let the word of Christ dwell in you richly, teach and admonish one another in all wisdom, and sing psalms and hymns and spiritual songs with thankfulness in your hearts to God." (Colossians 3:16)

"As it is, there are many parts, yet one body. The eye can not say to the hand, 'I have no need of you,' nor again the head to the feet, 'I have no need of you'.... If one member suffers, all suffer together; if one member is honored, all rejoice together." (1 Corinthians 12:20-21, 26)

MAKING A CHOICE

We do not choose to join the church; God chooses us. But we are faced with the problem of choosing between denominations and congregations, which are more or less helpful in promoting our life in Christ. The choice, in fact, may be between what is genuine and what is sham. Our Lord warns against false teachers "who come to you in sheep's clothing but inwardly are ravenous wolves," and people who prophesy in his name but are unknown to him. (Matthew 7:15, 21-23) Religious teachers must be put to a test. "Beloved, do not believe every spirit, but test the spirits to see whether they are of God." (1 John 4:1) St. Paul praised the Christians at Berea because they examined the Scriptures to see if what he taught was true.

Loyalty to the word and spirit of Christ our Lord and Savior must be the determining factor in our choice of a denomination or congregation and not the personality of the preacher, or sociableness of the members, or any other purely human consideration. What is essential to the fellowship of Christians is the preaching of the Gospel and the administration of the sacraments according to his command.

THE CHRISTIAN MINISTRY

The Christian ministry is a divine institution. The Holy Spirit appoints pastors to be guardians of the flock and to feed the church of the Lord. (Acts 20:28) The ascended Christ provides the church with pastors and teachers for building up his body. "His gifts were that some should be apostles, some prophets, some evangelists, some pastors and teachers, to equip the saints for the work of ministry, for building up the body of Christ." (Ephesians 4:11-12) the duty to preach the Gospel and administer the sacraments, which God has enjoined upon each Christian, is performed publicly and by proxy through called and ordained pastors. Pastors not only preach to the members of the congregation, they preach for them. They administer the sacraments and perform all the duties of their sacred office not only in their interest but also in their behalf. All the work of the congregation performed by its pastors, teachers and officers is your responsibility when you become a member. The blessedness and joy are yours, too. It is all your business, your highest interest in life, supported by your gifts, prayers and best efforts.

The term pastor, most commonly used by Lutheran people, emphasizes the minister's office as a shepherd and guardian of Christ's flock. Members of the congregation regard their pastor as their confidant and advisor in spiritual matters.

CHURCH MEMBERS

For their own sakes as well as for the well-being of the church, church members are required to be faithful in their use of the word of God and the sacraments, to share in the responsibility of church work, and support the church financially according to their ability, "not reluctantly or under compulsion, for God loves a cheerful giver." (2 Corinthians 9:7) What we put into the church in terms of interest and service will be the measure not only of what shall get out of it but also of what others will get out of us. "So then, as we have opportunity, let us do good to all men, and especially to those of the household of faith." (Galatians 6:10)

Lutheran Christians

Over seventy million people in Christendom bear the name *Lutheran*, despite Luther's plea that his followers call themselves Christians and not Lutherans. Until thirty-four years after his death (1546) his followers called themselves Evangelicals, from the late Latin word *evangelium* meaning Gospel, to emphasize the Gospel-centered thrust of the 16th century Reformation. "This one article," Luther said, "namely, faith in Christ, rules my heart. All my theological thoughts, day or night, proceed from this article, revolve about it, and always return to it." Calling one's self Lutheran implies subscribing to Luther's loyalty to the Gospel, especially as this is spelled out in the Lutheran confessions. It does not imply hero worship or appealing to Luther as a final authority in matters of Christian teaching.

The Lutheran Church in America

The Lutheran Church in America owes its origin to the immigration of Scandinavian and German Lutherans in the 17th, 18th and 19th centuries. Since each group retained its cultural background and language many separate regional church bodies, called synods, came into being. Gradually, as English became the common language and the cultural barriers vanished, communication among American Lutherans became possible and the problems of their differences could be addressed.

Eventually, three major Lutheran church bodies, embracing 95% of all the Lutherans in America, emerged. They are the Lutheran Church - Missouri Synod, originally named the Synod of Missouri, Ohio and Other States, founded in 1847; the Lutheran Church of America, originally the United Lutheran Church in America, founded in 1918; and the American Lutheran Church, founded in 1961. A further merger effected in 1987, known as the Evangelical Lutheran Church in America, brought together the Lutheran Church of America, the American Lutheran Church and the Association of Evangelical Lutheran Churches, an offshoot of the Missouri Synod, organized in 1977 and composed of moderates whose broader views on the meaning of the Bible's infallibility and requisites for Christian fellowship were officially condemned at the 1973 convention of the Missouri Synod. This new Lutheran church became the fourth largest Protestant denomination in the United States.

The Function of a Synod

A congregation's affiliation with a synod is necessary for carrying on the work of the Lord on a world-wide scale. To preach the Gospel in all the world, as Christ commanded, requires the training of pastors and teachers in theological colleges and seminaries, and sending out and supporting missionaries in our own country and in foreign lands. The largeness of the task requires the combined efforts and gifts of many congregations.

A synod is not to be regarded as a hierarchical body in which the affiliated congregations and its individual members are subordinate. It does not mandate but serves congregations in an advisory capacity. Our Lord said, "You have one master, the Christ." (Matthew 23:10)

Talking It Over

Use each of the following statements and questions as a basis for discussion.

1. What does *church* mean in the New Testament?

2. Why is the church called "the communion of saints"?

3. How can the church be both united and divided?

4. —the three concerns of the church

5. Why is being a Christian without being a member of the church not possible?

6. Why does a Christian seek the fellowship of a Christian congregation?

7. On what basis should the choice of a congregation or denomination be made?

8. —what faithful pastors do for their people

9. What characterizes a faithful congregation member?

True and False Statements

Circle the letter **T** for true statements and the letter **F** for false statements.

T F 1. The church is the only society of people on earth created by God.

T F 2. There are some Christians who are not members of the Christian church.

T F 3. In the New Testament church always means Christian people.

T F 4. There are many hypocrites in the church.

T F 5. God has left it to people to build the church.

T F 6. All members of the church are saints.

T F 7. The church, like its individual members, is both holy and unholy.

T F 8. The church seems to be but is not really divided.

T F 9. The unity of the church is disturbed by Christian people who insist on the correctness of their teachings.

T F   10. If all Christians would fully agree in their interpretation of the Bible there would be perfect unity in the church.

T F   11. To speak the truth lovelessly is as bad as not speaking the truth.

T F   12. More good than harm results from the fact that there are numerous Christian denominations.

T F   13. People cannot choose to join the church but they can choose not to join.

T F   14. One should be in full agreement with everything a congregation teaches and practices before joining it.

T F   15. The Bible blames false teachers for factions and divisions of the church.

T F   16. The New Testament takes it for granted that Christians are members of a Christian congregation.

T F   17. Being a member of a Christian congregation means being a member of the church.

T F   18. The growth of the church is a matter of statistics.

T F   19. Our Lord ministers to people today through his body, the church.

T F   20. Christians can not be expected to tithe (give ten percent of their income to the church) as was required of people in the Old Testament times.

T F   21. Every Christian is commanded to preach the Gospel and administer the sacraments.

T F   22. We should think of pastors primarily as persons appointed by God to serve our spiritual needs.

T F   23. A synod is a human device to carry out our Lord's command to preach the Gospel in all the world.

For Further Study

In making a choice about which congregation to join, rate the following considerations in the order of their importance.

____ Proximity to your home
____ Friendliness of the members
____ Personality of the pastor
____ Well-structured and meaningful order of service
____ Interesting sermons

____ Administration of the sacraments according to New Testament teaching
____ Christ-centered teaching
____ Organizations which afford opportunity for fellowship and service.

Bible Reading

St. Paul's Epistle to the Ephesians

A Prayer for the Church

Gracious Father,
>   we humbly beseech you for the whole church
>   throughout the world.
Fill it with all truth,
>   and in all truth with all peace.
> Where it is corrupt, purify it.
> Where it is in error, direct it.
> Where it is superstitious, cleanse it.
> Where anything is amiss, reform it.
> Where it is right, strengthen and confirm it.
> Where it is in want, furnish it.
> Where it is divided and rent assunder,
>   heal the breaches:
through Jesus Christ, our Lord.

14

OLY COMMUNION —
THE SACRAMENT OF LIFE

PREVIEW

All of the blessings of life with God that can be enjoyed on earth are offered to Christians in the spiritual banquet called Holy Communion or the Lord's Supper. We shall discuss the various names for this sacrament, under what circumstances Christ instituted it, how it is related to the major Old Testament festival of the Passover, the basic truths about its significance, and who is worthy to partake of it.

The lesson and book will conclude with a discussion of everlasting life and what it means for Christians to live in hope.

Various Names for Holy Communion

The New Testament has four accounts of our Lord's institution of Holy Communion (Matthew 26:26-29; Mark 14:22-25; Luke 22:14-20; I Corinthians 11:23-26). See page 146 for St. Paul's account which, because it is the most detailed, has found its way into the liturgy of the church.

The meaning and purpose of Holy Communion are indicated in a measure by the names by which it is known.

It is called THE SACRAMENT OF THE ALTAR. Along with Baptism it is a chief sacrament of the church because it was instituted by our Lord and offers the blessings of his redemptive work. It is the sacrament of the altar because it is celebrated at the altar of a house of worship. It must be added, however, that it is also administered to the sick and shut-ins in homes and hospitals.

It is called THE LORD'S SUPPER and THE LORD'S TABLE. Our Lord provides the food and is the host at this meal. The word supper reminds us that it was at an evening meal that he instituted this sacrament. The lighting of candles on the altar before the sacrament is celebrated serves to remind us of this.

It is called HOLY COMMUNION because it brings us together with Christ, our Lord, and with all who share this heavenly meal with us.

It is called EUCHARIST, which means thanksgiving, because, after the example of our Lord (1 Corinthians 11:24), Christians give thanks for the food which God provides for their bodies and souls.

The word MASS, used by many Christians, is probably derived from the practice in the early Christian church of dismissing from the service before its celebration persons who were not eligible to receive the sacrament.

The Historical Setting

It was in an upper room of a house in Jerusalem (Luke 22:12) and on the night that Judas betrayed him (1 Corinthians 11:23) that our Lord instituted Holy Communion. The church celebrates its institution on Maundy Thursday, the day before Good Friday when it commenorates his death on the cross.

The same night in the upper room our Lord gave the disciples an unforgettable example of humble service by washing their feet. (John 13:1-15) He also let Judas know, in a cryptic manner that revealed his great charity, that he was aware of his act of betrayal. (John 13:21-30)

The Relation Between Holy Communion and the Passover

Significant for our understanding of Holy Communion is the fact that it is intimately associated with the Jewish Passover. It was to eat the Passover that our Lord met with his disciples in the upper room. (Luke 22:7-13) It was at the Passover table that he instituted his new sacrament. In the Christian church the Old Testament Passover finds its fulfillment in the celebration of Holy Communion which has supplanted it. The Passover was the celebration of the old covenant between God and his people Israel; Holy Communion is the celebration of the new covenant between God and his church, the new Israel.

The Passover celebrated the great redemptive act of God which delivered the Israelites from their slavery in Egypt so that they might be his people and he their God. The blood of the sacrificial lamb with which they marked their doorposts, according to God's command, was the signal to the avenging angel, on his mission to slay all the first-born in the land, to pass over them. (Exodus 12:21-32) In Holy Communion, Christians celebrate their deliverance from slavery to sin and death through Christ, the Paschal lamb, who offered his body and shed his blood for them. An Easter hymn by Luther puts it this way:

> Here the true Paschal lamb we see,
> Whom God so freely gave us;
> He died on the accursed tree —
> So strong his love to save us.
> See, his blood now marks our door;
> Faith points to it, death passes o'er,
> And Satan can not harm us. Alleluia!

God's command regarding the Paschal lamb was not only that its blood be used to mark the Israelites' doorposts but also that it be eaten. (Exodus 12:3-8) To affirm that he is the Paschal lamb whom God sacrificed for our salvation, our Lord likewise offers us his body and blood given and shed for us as food to eat and drink. Jesus said, "Truly, truly, I say to you, unless you eat the flesh of the Son of man and drink his blood, you have no life in you; he who eats my flesh and drinks my blood has eternal life." (John 6:53-54)

Besides the sacrificial lamb the Passover meal included unleavened bread (which could be quickly baked and kept longer and therefore best served the needs of the Israelites in their hasty flight from Egypt), bitter herbs (which had to be chewed because the bondage of Egypt was bitter and hard), and wine which was ceremoniously drunk at specified times during the meal. Thus the Israelites not only remembered but relived the story of their deliverance at the hands of their almighty, gracious and ever-present God. Christians celebrate Holy Communion, according to their Lord's command, in remembrance of him whose help can always be counted on because his body and blood were broken and shed for them.

Basic Truths about Holy Communion

The rich meaning of Holy Communion can be expressed in a variety of terms. On the basis of the New Testament we have chosen the following: remembrance, proclamation, sacrifice, fellowship, thanksgiving and expectation.

HOLY COMMUNION AS A MEMORIAL SUPPER

Our Lord said, "Do this in remembrance of me." The breaking of bread and the pouring out of wine bring to mind that we owe our forgiveness and life to the body and blood that our Lord gave and shed for us on the cross.

The remembrance, however, contrary to our use of the word, is not of something or someone absent. It is a remembrance by which we experience anew his presence and the blessings of his sacrificial death.

HOLY COMMUNION AS AN ACT OF PROCLAMATION

By partaking of Holy Communion in a public service Christians let the world know that they are Christ's people. By their action they proclaim their common faith in Christ, "the Lamb of God who takes away the sin of the word!" (John 1:29) St. Paul says, "As often as you eat this bread and drink the cup, you proclaim the Lord's death until he comes." (1 Corinthians 11:26)

HOLY COMMUNION AS THE SACRAMENT OF SACRIFICE

The sacrificial death of Christ brought to an end all the sacrifices of the temple required under the old covenant. Their meaning and purpose were fulfilled, or fully realized, in the once-for-all sacrifice of the Son of God on the altar of the Cross. "By a single offering he has perfected for all time those who are sanctified." (Hebrews 10:14) Sacrifice is essential to all religions. What is unique about Christianity is not that there is no sacrifice but that it is God and not a human being who offers the sacrifice. By proclaiming the death of Christ communicants glory in an effective and perfect sacrifice which makes any further sacrifices for sin not only useless but insulting to God.

The only sacrifice required by Christians who celebrate Christ's sacrifice is the sacrifice of praise performed both by our lips and deeds. "Through him [Christ] let us continually offer up a sacrifice of praise to God, that is, the fruit of lips that acknowledge his name." (Hebrews 13:15) We do not in Holy Communion look at the sacrifice of Christ as we look at a picture on the wall. His sacrificial love controls us and makes us want to live and die for others with and for him. "He died for all, that those who live might live no longer for themselves but for him who for their sake died and rose again." (2 Corinthians 5:15)

HOLY COMMUNION AS THE SACRAMENT OF FELLOWSHIP

Eating the sacrifices of animals or food which they offered to God meant to the Israelites enjoying the close fellowship of sitting down with God at his table. Eating and drinking the bread and wine in Holy Communion similarly means entering into an intimate fellowship with Christ. "The cup of blessing which we bless, is it not a participation in the blood of Christ? The bread which we break, is it not a participation in the body of Christ?" (1 Corinthians 10:16) Eating and drinking the sacramental bread and wine means union with Christ's whole person. In Holy Communion he gives himself to us so that we are identified with him. St. Paul warns against a thoughtless and faithless use of the sacrament by saying, "Whoever, therefore, eats the bread or drinks the cup of the Lord in an unworthy manner will be guilty of profaning the body and blood of the Lord. Let a man examine himself and so eat of the bread and drink of the cup. For anyone who eats and drinks without discerning the body eat and drink judgment upon himself." (1 Corinthians 11:27-29)

The mystery of Holy Communion is the mystery of Christ's presence. No attempt should be made to solve it. To change the words of our Lord, "This is my body," to,

"This represents my body," may solve the mystery but it also removes his self-giving presence. Partaking of Holy Communion is an exercise in faith which needs strengthening for the many riddles of life.

Neither is the mystery the miracle in what happens to the bread and wine through a human act of consecration. It is in what happens within us when, by eating, drinking and believing, the body and blood of the Lord, his whole person, is given to us so that we can say with St. Paul, "It is no longer I who live, but Christ who lives in me; and the life I now live in the flesh I live by faith in the Son of God, who loved me and gave himself for me." (Galatians 2:20-21)

Life with God is most fully realized on earth in Holy Communion. With the bread and wine we receive the body and blood of Christ given and shed for the remission of our sins. "Where there is forgiveness," as Luther says, "there is life and salvation." If sin disrupts communion with God, forgiveness restores it. In the giving of himself to us in Holy Communion we immediately enjoy the fruit of forgiveness, which is fellowship with him who said, "I and the Father are one." (John 10:30)

Holy Communion also nourishes the fellowship of believers among themselves. The bond which unites Christian people is Christ himself, whose life they share in the sacrament. "Because there is one bread, we who are many are one body, for we all partake of the one bread." (1 Corinthians 10:17) Unfailingly, as Christ draws believers nearer to himself he draws them nearer to each other. The use of a single bread and a common cup, by our Lord in the upper room and in many congregations today, symbolizes the oneness of believers.

HOLY COMMUNION AS THE SACRAMENT OF THANKSGIVING

Holy Communion is sometimes called the Eucharist, which means thanksgiving. As our Lord gave thanks before he broke the bread in the upper room, so we too give thanks for his gifts of bread and wine in the sacrament and in daily life. Above all, we thank him for giving us himself. For all the sorrow that must attend the contemplation of our sins which brought about his death on the Cross, the dominant mood of communicants is joyful thanksgiving. Worshipers approach the Lord's Table with its heavenly food, with eager, grateful and happy hearts.

HOLY COMMUNION AS THE SACRAMENT OF EXPECTATION

Christians partake of Holy Communion in anticipation of the second coming of Christ and as a foretaste of the banquet they will enjoy in the kingdom of heaven where, in the words of an old Communion prayer, "we shall eat of the eternal manna and drink of the river of his pleasure forevermore." "As often as you eat this bread and drink the cup, you proclaim the Lord's death until he comes." (1 Corinthians 11:26) Jesus said to the disciples in the upper room, "As my Father assigned to me, a kingdom, that you may eat and drink at my table in my kingdom." (Luke 22:29-30)

The Worthy Communicant

See Luther's answer on page 138 to the question, "When is a person rightly prepared to receive this sacrament?"

1. Worthiness is a matter of the spirit and not of the body.

2. Worthy communicants acknowledge their unworthiness. They realize their sinfulness and need of forgiveness.

3. They have faith in the words, "Given and shed for you for the remission of sins."

4. They are able and willing to examine themselves. (1 Corinthians 11:29) They say yes to the questions:

    "Do I acknowledge my sins?"
    "Do I believe in Christ, my Savior?"
    "Do I intend to amend my sinful life?"

5. They discern the Lord's body (recognize Christ's presence in the sacrament) (1 Corinthians 11:29)

COMMUNING FREQUENTLY

The words of our Lord, "Do this, as often as you drink it, in remembrance of me," assume that Christians will partake of this sacrament frequently, or as often as they have the opportunity to do so. Could there ever be a time in their life when they would not desire the assurance of Christ's forgiveness and presence?

THE FAMILY MEAL

The Lord's Supper is the family meal of believers. Its purpose is not to make a Christian of one who is not a Christian, but to nourish the faith of those who are already Christians. It presupposes penitence, faith and fellowship with Christ and other Christians. The invitation to the Lord's Supper is extended to baptized Christians who desire and are prepared to receive Christ's forgiveness and ongoing presence in their lives. (See Luther's instruction on Holy Communion, page 138.)

A Prayer for Maundy Thursday

O Lord God,
who left us, in a wonderful sacrament,
a memorial of your Passion,
grant that we may so use this sacrament
of your body and blood
that the fruits of your redemption
may continually be manifest in us.

Life Everlasting

Life with the eternal God and with his Son, Jesus Christ, who died and is alive forevermore (Revelation 1:18), could never be anything less than everlasting life. Physical death does not destroy or even interrupt it. Our Lord said, "I am the resurrection and the life; he who believes in me, though he die, yet shall he live, and whoever lives and believes in me shall never die." (John 11:25-26) Life with God is as endless as the love of God in Christ Jesus from which nothing, not even death, can separate us. (Romans 8:38-39)

Life everlasting not only follows the resurrection of the body, as the Apostles' and Nicene creeds might seem to suggest. It also precedes it. It begins at baptism when we are born of water and the Spirit and enter the kingdom of God (John 3:5) or when faith in Christ begins. Jesus said, "Truly, truly, I say to you he who believes has eternal life." (John 6:47)

Christians expectantly await the visible return of their Lord to raise them from death and take them to heaven, where they shall fully enjoy their vision of him and their likeness with him, for which their earthly life prepares and trains them. "Beloved, we are God's children now; it does not yet appear what we shall be, but we know that when he appears we shall be like him, for we shall see him as he is." (1 John 3:2)

WE LIVE IN HOPE

Christian hope, so far from being mere wishful thinking, is a living hope guaranteed by God, who raised his Son from death and gave us the Holy Spirit as a down-payment on our inheritance. "In him [Christ] you also, who have heard the word of truth, the gospel of your salvation, and have believed in him, were sealed with the promises of the Holy Spirit, which is the guarantee of our inheritance until we acquire possession of it, to the praise of his glory." (Ephesians 1:13-14)

This glorious hope (1) sustains Christians in the sufferings of this life, (2) determines their choices and investments, (3) removes for them the sting of death and (4) makes it the door to eternal bliss.

1. "I consider that the sufferings of this present time are not worth comparing with the glory that is to be revealed to us." (Romans 8:18)

2. "Do not lay up for yourselves treasures on earth, where moth and rust consume and where thieves break in and steal, but lay up for yourselves treasures in heaven, where neither moth nor rust consumes and where thieves do not break in and steal." (Matthew 6:19-20)

3. "For this perishable nature must put on the imperishable, and this mortal nature

must put on immortality. When the perishable puts on the imperishable, and the mortal puts on immortality, then shall come to pass the saying that is written: Death is swallowed up in victory. O death, where is thy victory? O death, where is thy sting? The sting of death is sin and the power of sin is the law. But thanks be to God who gives us the victory through our Lord Jesus Christ." (1 Corinthians 15:53-57)

4. "Therefore are they before the throne of God, and serve him day and night within his temple; and he who sits upon the throne will shelter them with his presence. They shall hunger no more, neither thirst any more; the sun shall not strike them, nor any scorching heat. For the Lamb in the midst of the throne will be their shepherd, and he will guide them to springs of living water; and God will wipe away every tear from their eyes." (Revelation 7:15-17)

THE ROAD WE HAVE TRAVELED

Genesis begins with a couple created by God in a world that sin had never entered. Revelation ends with the people God re-created entering through the gates of the city in a new world from which sin has been forever banished. Genesis begins with God visiting Adam and Eve in the cool of the day to commune with them. Revelation ends with God establishing his permanent dwelling place in the midst of his redeemed people. Genesis begins with no tears ever falling, no pain or death ever known. Revelation ends with all tears forever wiped away, pain and death eternally abolished. All that was lost through sin has been restored in full through Christ, our Lord.

This is the life — life with God —
enjoyed by our first parents in paradise,
lost through sin,
restored by Christ,
revealed in sacred scriptures,
implanted by the Holy Spirit,
accepted by faith,
entered upon through Holy Baptism,
expressed in prayer, worship and love for people,
found in the church,
nurtured by the word of God and Holy Communion,
begun on earth and continuing forever in the bliss of heaven.

Talking It Over

Use each of the following statements and questions as a basis for discussion.

1. What are some different names for Holy Communion and what do they indicate about its meaning and purpose?

2. What events, besides the institution of Holy Communion, are associated with the upper room?

3. —the close relationship between Holy Communion and the Old Testament Passover

4. —the six words which bring to light the meaning and purpose of the sacrament Holy Communion

5. St. Paul admonishes Christians to examine themselves before partaking of Holy Communion. What questions must they ask themselves?

6. How is Christian hope different from the usual hopes of people?

7. How does the hope of Christians affect their daily lives?

True and False Statements

Circle the letter **T** for true statements and the letter **F** for false statements.

T F 1. The communion in Holy Communion is a coming together with Christ and with other Christians.

T F 2. Christianity is different from other religions because it has nothing to say about a sacrificial offering for sin.

T F 3. In Holy Communion, Christians remember their Lord in the same way that citizens of the United States remember George Washington on his birthday.

T F 4. One reason Christians celebrate Holy Communion is to tell the world that they believe in Christ.

T F 5. No sacrifice of any kind is required of believers in Christ.

T F 6. In Holy Communion, the believer receives forgiveness for past sins but not for sins not yet committed.

T F 7. The words of our Lord, "This is my body," should not be taken literally.

T F 8. Holy Communion does not further unity among Christians but reminds them that they are one in Christ.

T F 9. Holy Communion tends to become meaningless to people who partake of it too frequently.

T F 10. Christians will sometimes find that they are in no mood to partake of Holy Communion.

T F 11. To be worthy to partake of Holy Communion we must confess that we are unworthy.

T F 12. To partake of Holy Communion worthily requires a strong faith.

T F 13. As everyone is welcome to attend public worship, so everyone should be welcomed at the Lord's Table.

T F 14. Remembering their sins which caused Christ's death, Christians are bound to feel sad when they partake of Holy Communion.

T F 15. Eternal life in the New Testament means life in heaven.

T F 16. Physical death, even for the believer, is punishment for sin.

T F 17. Since Christ removed the sting of death believers are naturally anxious to die.

T F 18. Everyone should find comfort in the fact that Christ will raise him or her from death on Judgment Day.

T F 19. Heaven is best described as the full enjoyment of God's presence.

T F 20. Heaven describes a bliss which people on earth can know nothing of.

T F 21. The element of certainty distinguishes Christian hope from every other kind of hope.

Bible Reading

The Gospel of Luke
Chapters 15-24

A Prayer That Nothing May Separate Us from God's Love

God of all grace,
      you sent your Son, our Savior Jesus Christ,
      to bring life and immortality to light.
We give you thanks
      because by his death Jesus destroyed the power of
      death and by his resurrection has opened the kingdom
      of heaven to all believers.
Make us certain
      that because he lives we shall live also,
      and that neither death nor life, nor things
      present nor things to come shall be able to
      separate us from your love
         which is in Christ Jesus our Lord.

"That which we have seen and heard we proclaim also to you, so that you may have fellowship with us; and our fellowship is with the Father and with his Son Jesus Christ."

1 John 1:3

THE SMALL CATECHISM

by Martin Luther

The Ten Commandments

I am the Lord your God.

The First Commandment

You shall have no other gods.

What does this mean for us?

We are to fear, love and trust God above anything else.

The Second Commandment

You shall not take the name of the Lord your God in vain.

What does this mean for us?

We are to fear and love God so that we do not use His name to curse, swear, lie, *witchcraft* or deceive, but call on Him in prayer, praise and thanksgiving.

The Third Commandment

Remember the Sabbath Day, to keep it holy.

What does this mean for us?

We are to fear and love God so that we do not neglect His word and the preaching of it, but regard it as holy and gladly hear and learn it.

The Fourth Commandment

Honor your father and your mother.

What does this mean for us?

We are to fear and love God so that we do not despise or anger our parents and others in authority, but respect, obey, love and serve them.

The Fifth Commandment

You shall not kill.

What does this mean for us?

We are to fear and love God so that we do not hurt our neighbor in any way, but help him in all his physical needs.

The Sixth Commandment

You shall not commit adultery.

What does this mean for us?

We are to fear and love God so that in matters of sex our words and conduct are pure and honorable, and husband and wife love and respect each other.

The Seventh Commandment

You shall not steal.

What does this mean for us?

We are to fear and love God so that we do not take our neighbor's money or property, or get them in any dishonest way, but help him to improve and protect his property and means of making a living.

The Eighth Commandment

You shall not bear false witness against your neighbor.

What does this mean for us?

We are to fear and love God so that we do not betray, slander, or lie about our neighbor, but defend him, speak well of him and explain his actions in the kindest way.

The Ninth Commandment

You shall not covet your neighbor's house.

What does this mean for us?

We are to fear and love God so that we do not desire to get our neighbor's possessions by scheming, or by pretending to have a right to them, but always help him keep what is his.

The Tenth Commandment

You shall not covet your neighbor's wife, or his manservant, or his maidservant, or his cattle, or anything that is your neighbor's.

What does this mean for us?

We are to fear and love God so that we do not tempt or coax away from our neighbor his wife or his workers, but encourage them to remain loyal.

What does God say of all these commandments?

He says:

"I, the Lord your God, am a jealous God, visiting the iniquity of the fathers upon the children to the third and fourth generation of those who hate Me, but showing steadfast love to thousands of those who love Me and keep My commandments."

What does this mean for us?

God warns that He will punish all who break these commandments. Therefore we are to fear His wrath and not disobey Him. But He promises grace and every blessing to all who keep these commandments. Therefore we are to love and trust Him, and gladly do what He commands.

The Apostles' Creed

The First Article

I believe in God the Father Almighty, Maker of heaven and earth.

What does this mean?

I believe that God has created me and all that exists. He has given me and still preserves my body and soul with all their powers.

He provides me with food and clothing, home and family, daily work, and all I need from day to day. God also protects me in time of danger and guards me from every evil.

All this He does out of fatherly and divine goodness and mercy, though I do not deserve it. Therefore I surely ought to thank and praise, serve and obey Him.

This is most certainly true.

The Second Article

And in Jesus Christ, His only Son, our Lord, who was conceived by the Holy Ghost, born of the Virgin Mary; suffered under Pontius Pilate, was crucified, dead, and buried; He descended into hell; the third day He rose again from the dead; He ascended into heaven, and sitteth on the right hand of God the Father Almighty; from thence He shall come to judge the quick and the dead.

What does this mean?

I believe that Jesus Christ—true God, Son of the Father from eternity, and true man, born of the Virgin Mary—is my Lord.

He has redeemed me, a lost and condemned person, saved me at great cost from sin, death, and the power of the devil—not with silver or gold, but with His holy and precious blood and His innocent suffering and death.

All this He has done that I may be His own, live under Him in His kingdom, and serve Him in everlasting righteousness, innocence and blessedness, just as He is risen from the dead and lives and rules eternally.

This is most certainly true.

The Third Article

I believe in the Holy Ghost; the holy Christian church, the communion of saints; the forgiveness of sins; the resurrection of the body; and the life everlasting. Amen.

What does this mean?

I believe that I cannot by my own understanding or effort believe in Jesus Christ, my Lord, or come to Him. But the Holy Spirit has called me through the Gospel, enlightened me with His gifts, and sanctified and kept me in the true faith.

In the same way He calls, gathers, enlightens and sanctifies the whole Christian church on earth, and keeps it united with Jesus Christ in the one true faith.

In this Christian church day after day He fully forgives my sins and the sins of all believers. On the last day He will raise me and all the dead and give me and all believers in Christ eternal life. This is most certainly true.

(For your convenience and reference, you will find The Nicene Creed printed on page 148.)

The Lord's Prayer

The Introduction

Our Father who art in heaven.

What does this mean?

Here God encourages us to believe that He is truly our Father and we are His children. We therefore are to pray to Him with complete confidence just as children speak to their loving father.

The First Petition

Hallowed be Thy name.

What does this mean?

God's name certainly is holy in itself, but we ask in this prayer that we may keep it holy.

When does this happen?

God's name is hallowed whenever His word is rightly taught and we as children of God live in harmony with it. Help us to do this, heavenly Father!

But anyone who teaches or lives contrary to the word of God dishonors God's name among us. Keep us from doing this, heavenly Father!

The Second Petition

Thy Kingdom come.

What does this mean?

God's kingdom comes indeed without our praying for it; but we ask in this prayer that it may come also to us.

When does this happen?

God's kingdom comes when our heavenly Father gives us His Holy Spirit, so that by His grace we believe His holy word and live a godly life on earth now and in heaven forever.

The Third Petition

Thy will be done on earth as it is in heaven.

What does this mean?

The good and gracious will of God is surely done without our prayer, but we ask in this prayer that it may be done also among us.

When does this happen?

God's will is done when He hinders and defeats every evil scheme and purpose of the devil, the world, and our sinful self, which would prevent us from keeping His name holy and would oppose the coming of His kingdom. And His will is done when He strengthens our faith and keeps us firm in His word as long as we live.

The Fourth Petition

Give us this day our daily bread.

What does this mean?

> God gives daily bread, even without our prayer, to all people, though sinful, but we ask in this prayer that He will help us to realize this and to receive our daily bread with thanks.

What is meant by "daily bread"?

> Daily bread includes everything needed for this life, such as food and clothing, home and property, work and income, a devoted family, an orderly community, good government, favorable weather, peace and health, a good name, and true friends and neighbors.

The Fifth Petition

> And forgive us our trespasses, as we forgive those who trespass against us.

What does this mean?

> We ask in this prayer that our Father in heaven would not hold our sins against us and because of them refuse to hear our prayer. And we pray that He would give us everything by grace, for we sin every day and deserve nothing but punishment.

> So we on our part will heartily forgive and gladly do good to those who sin against us.

The Sixth Petition

> And lead us not into temptation.

What does this mean?

> God tempts no one to sin, but we ask in this prayer that God would watch over us so that the devil, the world, and our sinful self may not deceive us and draw us into unbelief, despair, and other great and shameful sins.

> And we pray that even though we are so tempted we may still win the final victory.

The Seventh Petition

> But deliver us from evil.

What does this mean?

> We ask in this inclusive prayer that our heavenly Father would save us from every evil to body and soul, and at our last hour would mercifully take us from the troubles of this world to himself in heaven.

The Doxology
For Thine is the kingdom and the power and the glory forever and ever. Amen.

What does "Amen" mean?
Amen means *Yes, it shall be so.* We say Amen because we are certain that such petitions are pleasing to our Father in heaven. For He Himself has commanded us to pray in this way and has promised to hear us.

The Sacrament of Baptism

What is Baptism?
The sacrament of Baptism is not water only, but it is water used together with God's word and by His command.

What is this word?
In Matthew 28 our Lord Jesus Christ says: "Go therefore and make disciples of all nations, baptizing them in the name of the Father and of the Son and of the Holy Spirit."

What benefits does God give in Baptism?
In Baptism God forgives sin, delivers from death and the devil, and gives everlasting salvation to all who believe what He has promised.

What is God's promise?
In Mark 16 our Lord Jesus Christ says: "He who believes and is baptized will be saved; but he who does not believe will be condemned."

How can water do such great things?
It is not water that does these things, but God's word with the water and our trust in this word. Water by itself is only water, but with this word it is a life-giving water which by grace gives the new birth through the Holy Spirit.

St. Paul writes in Titus 3: "He saved us...in virtue of His own mercy, by the washing to regeneration and renewal in the Holy Spirit, which He poured out upon us richly through Jesus Christ, our Savior, so that we might be justified by His grace and become heirs in hope of eternal life. The saying is sure."

What does Baptism mean for daily living?
It means that our sinful self, with all its evil deeds and desires, should be drowned through daily repentance; and that day after day a new self should arise to live with God in righteousness and purity forever.

St. Paul writes in Romans 6: "We were buried therefore with Him by Baptism into death, so that as Christ was raised from the dead by the glory of the Father, we too might walk in newness of life."

The Sacrament of Holy Communion

What is Holy Communion?

It is the sacrament instituted by Christ Himself, in which He gives us His body and blood in and with the bread and wine.

What are the words of institution?

Our Lord Jesus Christ, in the night in which He was betrayed, took bread; and when He had given thanks, He broke it and gave it to His disciples, saying, "Take, eat; this is My body, which is given for you; this do in remembrance of Me."

After the same manner also He took the cup after supper, and when He had given thanks, He gave it to them, saying, "Drink of it, all of you; this cup is the new testament in My blood, which is shed for you, and for many, for the remission of sins; this do, as often as you drink it, in remembrance of Me."

What benefits do we receive from this sacrament?

The benefits of this sacrament are pointed out by the words, given and shed for you for the remission of sins. These words assure us that in the sacrament we receive forgiveness of sins, life, and salvation. For where there is forgiveness of sins, there is also life and salvation.

How can eating and drinking do all this?

It is not eating and drinking that does this, but the words, given and shed for you for the remission of sins. These words, along with eating and drinking, are the main thing in the sacrament. And whoever believes these words has exactly what they say, forgiveness of sins.

When is a person rightly prepared to receive this sacrament?

Fasting and other outward preparations serve a good purpose. However, that person is well prepared and worthy who believes these words, *given and shed for you for the remission of sins*. But anyone who does not believe these words, or doubts them, is neither prepared nor worthy, for the words *for you* require simply a believing heart.

The Office of the Keys

What is the "Office of the Keys?"

It is that authority which Christ gave to His church to forgive the sins of those who repent and to declare to those who do not repent that their sins are not forgiven.

What are the words of Christ?

Our Lord Jesus Christ said to His disciples, "Receive the Holy Spirit. If you forgive the sins of any, they are forgiven; if you retain the sins of any, they are retained." (John 20:23)

"Truly, I say to you, whatever you bind on earth shall be bound in heaven, and whatever you loose on earth shall be loosed in heaven." (Matthew 18:18)

What is private confession?

Private confession has two parts. First, we make a personal confession of sins to the pastor, and then we receive absolution, which means forgiveness as from God Himself. This absolution we should not doubt, but firmly believe that thereby our sins are forgiven before God in heaven.

What sins should we confess?

Before God we should confess that we are guilty of all sins, even those which are not known to us, as we do in the Lord's Prayer. But in private confession, as before the pastor, we should confess only those sins which trouble us in heart and mind.

What are such sins?

We can examine our everyday life according to the Ten Commandments—for example, how we act toward father or mother, son or daughter, husband or wife, or toward the people with whom we work, and so on. We may ask ourselves whether we have been disobedient or unfaithful, bad-tempered or dishonest, or whether we have hurt anyone by word or deed.

How might we confess our sins privately?

We may say that we wish to confess our sins and to receive absolution in God's name. We may begin by saying, "I, a poor sinner, confess before God that I am guilty of many sins." Then we should name the sins that trouble us. We may close the confession with the words, "I repent of all these sins and pray for mercy. I promise to do better with God's help."

What if we are not troubled by any special sins?

We should not torture ourselves with imaginary sins. If we cannot think of any sins to confess (which would hardly ever happen), we need not name any in particular, but may receive absolution because we have already made a general confession to God.

How may we be assured of forgiveness?

The pastor may pronounce the absolution by saying, "By the authority of our Lord Jesus Christ I forgive you your sins in the name of the Father and of the Son and of the Holy Spirit. Amen."

Those who are heavily burdened in conscience the pastor may comfort and encourage with further assurances from God's Word.

The Nicene Creed

We believe in one God, the Father, the Almighty, maker of heaven and earth, of all that is, seen and unseen.

We believe in one Lord, Jesus Christ, the only Son of God, eternally begotten of the Father, God from God, Light from Light, true God from true God, begotten, not made, of one Being with the Father. Through him all things were made. For us and for our salvation he came down from heaven; by the power of the Holy Spirit he became incarnate from the virgin Mary, and was made man.

For our sake he was crucified under Pontius Pilate; he suffered death and was buried. On the third day he rose again in accordance with the Scriptures; he ascended into heaven and is seated at the right hand of the Father.

He will come again in glory to judge the living and the dead, and his kingdom will have no end.

We believe in the Holy Spirit, the Lord, the giver of life, who proceeds from the Father and the Son. With the Father and the Son he is worshiped and glorified. He has spoken through the prophets. We believe in one holy catholic and apostolic Church. We acknowledge one Baptism for the forgiveness of sins. We look for the resurrection of the dead, and the life of the world to come. Amen.